Contents

www.camra.org.uk/books

© Campaign for Real Ales 2009

ISBN-10: 978-1-85249-257-1

A CIP catalogue record for this book is available from the British Library.

Printed and bound in the UK by Breckland Print - 01953 454699 www.brecklandprint.com

Compiler & Editor: Warren Wordsworth

Designed by: A4 Art - mail@a4art.org.uk

Editorial Team: Des O'Brien, Graham Freeman and Martin Ward.

We would like to thank the following; Ray Parker, for planning some of the earlier routes; Derek McDonald, for some of the historical notes; Roger Blackwell, for helping format the layouts of walks as featured on the web site. My father, Norman Wordsworth, for helping with proof reading and editing. Philip Tolley for supplying archive material. Lastly, to all the countless people who have turned up and joined me to survey the market towns.

Foreword

Like many a project this started small and grew. In January 2003 a small group visited Great Yarmouth & Gorleston and surveyed many of the pubs there and as a result in April 2003 we produced a mini guide of the area which concentrated on the best pubs selling real ale.

Later in 2003 our committee considered a similar survey of Norwich Pubs. However, it was soon realised that it was not possible to produce a comprehensive guide and instead as a compromise we agreed to produce a series of "Pub Walks". Accordingly routes were surveyed and six pub walks were published in leaflet form and sold as leaflet packs at the 2004 Norwich Beer Festival.

Following this success the range of "Pub Walks" was extended into the county, to the market towns of Attleborough, Wells, Diss, Cromer, Sheringham, (including The North Norfolk Railway), Wymondham, Fakenham, Dereham, and Gt Yarmouth., plus walks on The Bure Valley Railway that incorporate Aylsham, Coltishall and Wroxham and a rural ramble round Cley, Wiveton and Blakeney.

Together with updated and revised Norwich Walks, this new guide now contains eighteen Pub Walks, seven in Norwich and eleven in the county.

Our "Pub Walks" are far from complete. In a later edition I hope to include towns such as Harleston, North Walsham, & Gorleston, and also to include some 'village hopping routes' similar to the Cley, Wiveton & Blakeney walk.

Lastly I would welcome any suggestions or ideas please don't hesitate to contact me on w.wordsworth@ntlworld.com or by post to 16 Grove Avenue, Norwich NR1 2QD

Warren Wordsworth January 2009.

WHATEVER YOU DO, TAKE PRIDE.

Local Breweries

During the decade of the 1960s all the well known local breweries in Norwich were taken over by the national brewing giant Watneys. Great Yarmouth fared no better with the loss of its only brewery, Lacons by Whitbreds which finally closed in 1968. In Norwich by 1970, Watneys had closed all Norwich breweries except The King Street Brewery where their Norfolk brewing was centralised. It was not until the early 1980s that a few independent brewers started to emerge. Grand Metropolitan, who by this time owned Watneys, closed their Norwich brewery in 1984.

This paved the way for new independents and micros to flourish. Since then the number of local brewers has mushroomed. Norfolk now boasts a great diversity of brewers with over twenty five small independent and micro breweries. Thus when you visit pubs listed in this guide you will encounter a substantial range of excellent ales brewed locally, some even on the premises. Space does not allow a comprehensive list of all local breweries and local beers, but this section includes most of the more popular local brewers and beers that are supplied to the pubs listed in this guide. I have also included details of a few breweries and beers brewed in neighbouring counties whose beers are commonly found in Norfolk Pubs. Even though not brewed in this county they are never the less regarded as local beers and therefore included.

To find out more details of the breweries that are listed below and their ranges of beers you may wish to consult the current copy of CAMRA's "Good Beer Guide", or visit their websites as given below.

FULLER'S - Fuller, Smith & Turner plc
Griffin Brewery, Chiswick Lane South, London W4 2QB
Tel: 020 8996 2000 Website www.fullers.co.uk
Fuller's, London's last remaining regional brewer, is based at the historic Griffin Brewery, Chiswick. Located between the serenity of the River Thames and the hustle and bustle of the Hogarth Roundabout, Fuller's have been brewing quality beers and running excellent pubs since 1845. Although the majority of Fuller's pubs are located in the south-east, it is possible to sample a pint of Fuller's finest in the Norfolk area in many excellent free houses choosing to stock these superb beers. So if you are lucky enough to see Fuller's on the bar, then why not give them a try?
London Pride (4.1%). A well-known and well-loved classic premium ale. Rich and smooth, London Pride has a good malty base with an excellent blend of hop character, resulting in an easy drinking beer with great body and a fruity, satisfying finish.
ESB (5.5%) Winner of many awards around the world, including three times Champion Beer of Britain. This famous strong ale is deep red colour, with a powerful malt base complemented by a full array of hop flavours in perfect balance.
Chiswick Bitter (3.5%) A former CAMRA champion Beer of Britain, Chiswick Bitter is a light and refreshing beer with biscuity malt and crisp hop flavours. Extra hops are added to the cask to give a wonderfully distinctive hoppy aroma and a lasting bitterness in the finish.
Discovery, (3.9%) Brewed using a unique blend of malted barley and wheat for a delicious malty

taste bursting with rich, biscuity flavours. Liberty hops are added for a distinctive zesty character and fruity bite, whilst Saaz hops add a gentle bitter taste for a clean, refreshing finish.

Gales HSB (4.8%), A popular and distinctive premium beer, HSB is brewed with the finest malt and hops for a well-balanced character. A hint of Dundee cake on the nose leads to a rich, fruity taste and a silky smooth finish.

WOODFORDE'S NORFOLK ALES - Broadland Brewery, Woodbastwick, Norwich, Norfolk NR13 6SW. Tel 01603 720353   Website www.woodfordes.co.uk

Founded in 1981 on an industrial site in Drayton, Woodforde's, is now Norfolk's oldest brewery. Its name derives from Parson Woodforde, an 18th century clergyman who gained fame through writing his diaries which revealed his passion for food and good ales. In 1983 the brewery moved to the North Norfolk village of Erpingham opposite the Spread Eagle pub before another move to its present home "The Broadland Brewery" in Woodbastwick in 1989. The Fur & Feather pub, the brewery's tap opened in 1993. Since then it has undergone many expansions and is now the largest brewery in Norfolk supplying many outlets in Norfolk and beyond. Recently The Brewery Shop and Visitor Centre have been enlarged. Their beers have won a large number of both National and regional CAMRA awards.

Mardlers Mild (3.5%). Gentle, delicate sweet roasted malts combined with a low hopping rate make this traditional East Anglian Mild an ideal appetiser.

Wherry (3.8%). Fresh and zesty with crisp floral flavours. A background of sweet malt and a hoppy 'grapefruit' bitter finish characterises this champion beer.

Sundew (4.1%). Subtle golden beer - pale in colour and light on the palate with a distinctive hoppy Woodforde's finish. Deliciously golden and refreshing.

Norfolk Nog, (4.5%). Smooth, rich and rounded 'Old Ale' with a velvety texture and hints of chocolate, treacle and liquorice.

Nelson's Revenge (4.5%). Rich and floral aromas, sweet Norfolk malts and a burst of 'citrus' hops embody this mouth-watering premium beer.'

Admiral's Reserve, (5.0%). Solid and generous sweet fruit flavour create a complex and satisfying dark chestnut-coloured beer. Wonderfully, and dangerously, drinkable.

Headcracker (7%). Pale but strong and full-bodied. Carries an intricate combination of plums and damsons countered by an abundance of 'citrus' hopping.

WOLF BREWERY LTD - Rookery Farm, Silver Street, Besthorpe, Attleborough, Norfolk, NR17 2LD. Tel 01953 457775   Website www.wolfbrewery.com

The Wolf Brewery was established in 1996 by Wolfe Witham, who previously owned The Reindeer Brewery in Norwich. For most of its life it has been situated on old Gaymers cider factory site in Attleborough, although recently it has moved to a new site just to the south of Attleborough in Besthorpe. It is now the second largest brewery in Norfolk. The brewery supplies to many outlets in Norfolk and beyond. Their main range of range of cask beers are:-

Local Breweries

Golden Jackal 3.7% abv. A hoppy thirst-quenching golden session bitter, with a flowery nose and slightly citrus after-taste. The hop flavour lasts right through to the bottom of the glass.

Wolf Ale 3.9% Copper coloured ale with lots of bite! Goldings and Challenger hops combined with locally grown malt make this a glorious full bodied brew.

Coyote 4.3% A full-bodied premium straw coloured ale. Complex but well balanced mix of hops and malt leads onto a crisp well hopped finale.

Straw Dog 4.5% A pale and refreshing, this clear wheat beer is brewed in the German style. Soft German hops added to the brew give a wonderful aroma and slightly sweet taste to leave the imbiber wanting more!

Granny Wouldn't Like It 4.8% Dark red, rich and fruity. This mighty beer has many awards to its name. The swirling mix of flavours produces a complex but satisfying experience.

Woild Moild 4.8% A rich and fruity traditional Norfolk mild. Good balance of malt with liquorice bitterness and lots of chocolate malt. Dark ruby-red mild with a long lasting finish.

ADNAMS PLC. - Sole Bay Brewery, East Green, Southwold, Suffolk. IP18 6JW.
Tel 01502 727200   Website www.adnams.co.uk

Situated in the North Suffolk seaside resort of Southwold, Adnams is one of the oldest and most respected breweries in the east of England. You will find their beers in many of the pubs on these pub walks. The brewery has recently had a new eco friendly distribution house built nearby at Reydon. The beer you will encounter most frequently is 'Adnams Bitter' at 3.7%, their ever popular standard bitter. Other beers produced include, Broadside 4.7%, which is stronger malty ale and 'Explorer' 4.3%, a light hoppy beer. Adnams also produce a number of seasonal beers such as 'Oyster Stout' 4.3%; 'May Day', 5.0%; 'Regatta' 4.3%, brewed from June to August while brewed late in the year for Christmas are Old Ale; Yuletide 4.5% and Tally Ho', 7.0%.

GEORGE BATEMAN & SON LTD. - Salem Bridge Brewery, Wainfleet All Saints, Lincs PE24 4JE.
Tel 01754 880317   Website www.bateman.co.uk

Based in Lincolnshire, Bateman's has been brewing beer since 1874, and is another old well established family brewery. Most of their tied houses are in Lincolnshire and the East Midlands but they have recently bought tied houses in Norfolk They have five pubs in Norfolk, two of which The Kings Arms and Champion are featured in the Norwich pub walks. Their beer is also available as guest ale in several pubs in the Norfolk area. Their best known beers are Dark Mild 3.0%; XB Bitter 3.7%; XXXB 4.8% which is a strong bitter; Valiant, 4.2% a golden ale and 'Salem Porter' 4.7%. They also brew a number of seasonal ales.

BEESTON BREWERY - Fransham Road Farm, Beeston, Kings Lynn, Norfolk PE32 2LZ.
Tel 01328 700844

A newcomer to the Norfolk brewing scene, this micro brewery was opened in November 2006 by Mark Riches. They brew four beers, 'Afternoon Delight' 3.7% a light blond ale; 'Worth the Wait'

Local Breweries

4.2% a golden ale which won "Beer of the Festival" at the 2007 Norwich Beer Festival; 'On the Huh' 5.0% a stronger malty beer and most recently 'Norfolk Black' 5% a stout named after a local breed of turkey.

BLACKFRIARS BREWERY - The Courtyard, Main Cross Road Gt Yarmouth NR30 3NZ.
Tel 01493 850578 Website www.blackfriars-brewery.co.uk
Originally based in a small industrial unit in Gt Yarmouth, this brewery started in 2004. The brewery has recently moved to a new site which incorporates a shop and small museum. They have made big inroads in the free trade in Yarmouth and regularly supply some pubs in Norwich. Their 'Yarmouth Bitter' 3.8% won Beer of The Festival at Norwich Beer Festival in 2006. Other beers brewed include, 'Sygnus Bitter Gold' 4.0%, a hoppy grainy beer; 'Blackfriars Mild' 3.4%; 'Maritime' 5%, a premium bitter and 'Old Habit' 5.6%, a dark roasty malty beer. They also brew seasonal ales.

BUFFY'S BREWERY - Rectory Road, Tivetshall St Mary, Norfolk NR15 2DD.
Tel 01379 676523 Website www.buffys.co.uk
The brewery was established in 1993. Buffy's beers are available in a wide number of pubs in Norwich and in several Norfolk pubs including their own pub The Cherry Tree at Wicklewood where most of their range is usually available. Their beers include 'Buffy's Mild', 4.2%; 'Norwich Terrier', a light beer 3.6%; 'Buffy's Bitter' 3.9%, a traditional bitter that is their most popular beer; 'Polly's Folly', 4.3%; Hopleaf, 4.5%, which has a slightly spicy aroma; 'Mucky Duck' 4.5% a dark beer and Norwegian Blue, 4.9%.

CHALK HILL BREWERY - Rosary Road, Norwich, NR1 4DA. Tel 01603 477078
Website www.thecoachthorperoad.co.uk
The Chalk Hill Brewery which was founded in 1993 is a brewhouse pub situated at The Coach & Horses near Norwich Railway Station and featured in Norwich Pub Walk 2. Their beers are also sold at The Alexandra Tavern in Norwich Pub Walk 4. Their range includes 'Brewery Tap' 3.6%; 'CHB', 4.2%; 'Chalk Hill Gold' 4.3%; 'Dreadnought'; 4.9%, a strong malty brew, 'Flintknapper's Mild' 5%, a strong mild and 'Old Tackle' 5.6%, a strong sweet malty brew.

ELGOOD & SONS LTD - North Brink Brewery, Wisbech, Cambs, PE13 1LN.
Tel 01945 583160 Website www.elgoods-brewery.co.uk
This is another long established family brewer from Wisbech in Cambridgeshire, just over the Norfolk border. Most of the breweries tied estate is situated in the fenland areas of North Cambridgeshire, South Lincolnshire and West Norfolk. They have one pub in Norwich, The Reindeer, that is featured in Pub Walks 3 and 4 and their beers are also available as guest ales in many of the pubs featured in this guide. Their main beers include 'Black Dog '3.6%, one of the region's most popular milds; 'Cambridge', 3.8%, the breweries standard bitter; 'Golden Newt' 4.1%; 'Pageant', 4.3%; and 'Greyhound' 5.2%, a rich brown strong bitter. Elgood's also brew a number of seasonal ales.

Local Breweries

ELMTREE BEERS - The Stables, Mill Lane, Snetterton, Norfolk, NR16 2LQ.
Tel 07939 549241   Website www.elmtreebeers.co.uk

This brewery was established in early 2007. The main beers brewed include, Best Bitter 4.2%; Dark Horse 5%; Golden Pale Ale 5%; and Nightlght 5.7%, a dark mild which won champion beer at Norwich Beer Festival 2008.

FAT CAT BREWERY - The Shed, 98-100 Lawson Road, Norwich NR3 4LS.
Tel 01603 788508   Website www.fatcatpub.co.uk

This brewery was founded in September 2005 by Colin Keatley at The Shed, which is sister pub to his award winning Fat Cat pub featured in Walk 4.

Fat Cat Bitter 3.6%. is a straw coloured bitter with a distinct floral, spicy aroma from Cascade and Golding hops. The subtle blend of continental speciality malts with classic English pale malt gives a distinctive, slightly smoky taste, which blends well with the hop bitterness to give a spicy, yet well-balanced bitter.

Fat Cat Honey Ale 4.3%. is a mid-brown coloured ale, combining the full flavour of English pale and crystal malts with Norfolk honey, giving a sweetish, yet full-flavoured ale. The spicy notes of Cascade hops combine well with the honey to give a smooth finish, with a notable, hoppy bite.

Fat Cat Stout Cat 4.6%. is an attractively-coloured deep red/brown beer. The characteristic sweet, rich flavour of roast malt and molasses is well balanced with the pronounced hop flavour and aroma of classic English Fuggle hops.

Fat Cat Top Cat 4.8 % is a golden coloured pale ale, with a notable citrus/pine aroma from Cascade and Styrian hops. The well-balanced malty sweetness and spicy hop bitterness continues through to a long-lasting finish.

Fat Cat Marmalade Cat 5.5%. is a classic mid-brown coloured strong bitter, with a markedly bitter finish from the generous use of Styrian hops. Flavoursome English pale malt adds balance and a smooth finish, which lasts and lasts. Full-bodied, yet with an ease of drinking which belies its strength.

FRONT STREET - 45 Front Street, Binham, Fakenham, Norfolk, NR21 0AL.
Tel 01328 830297   Website www.frontstreetbrewery.co.uk

Beers are brewed at Binham Chequers pub in North Norfolk. The beer range includes Binham Cheer, 3.9%; Callums Ale 4.3% and Unity Strong 5%.

GRAIN BREWERY - South Farm, Alburgh, Harleston, Norfolk IP20 0BS.
Tel 01986 788884   Website www.grainbrewery.co.uk

Situated in South Norfolk this brewery started brewing in August 2006. Their range of cask ales include, 'Oak', 3.8%, their standard bitter; 'Blackwood Stout' 5%; 'Ported Porter', a creamy porter 5.2% and 'Tamarind' 5.5% which is a strong IPA. They also brew some seasonal ales. Their beers are available in some outlets in Norfolk and a brewery shop where bottled conditioned versions of their beers can be purchased was opened on the premises in July 2007.

grain
norfolk brewery

Local Breweries

GREEN JACK BREWERY - Triangle Tavern, 29 St Peters Street, Lowestoft, NR32 1QA.
Tel 01502 582711   Website www.green-jack.co.uk

Green Jack is a small micro brewery which started brewing in 2003 in Lowestoft. Beers brewed include 'Canary' 3.8%; 'Orange Wheat' 4.2%, which won 'Beer of the Festival' at the 2005 Norwich Beer Festival; 'Gone Fishing' 5.5%; and 'Ripper' 8.5% a very strong brew. To sample the full range you will have to travel to the Triangle Tavern in Lowestoft or The Locks Inn at Geldeston but some appear as guest ales in some of the pubs featured in this guide, particularly in the Yarmouth area.

GREENE KING PLC - Westgate Brewery, Bury St Edmunds, Suffolk, IP33 1QT.
Tel 01284 763222   Website www.greeneking.co.uk

Once listed as a large independent, Greene King first started brewing in 1799 and is now considered a National Brewer since the acquisition of Morland Brewery from Oxford, Ruddles Brewery from Rutland and more recently Ridleys of Chelmsford, Belhavens from Dunbar in Scotland and Hardys & Hansons from Kimberly near Nottingham in the East Midlands. Its tied estate nationally is now over 3,000 pubs. Greene King beers are found in numerous outlets in Norfolk including many of the pubs in this guide. The most common ones you will encounter are 'IPA' 3.6%;   and 'Abbot Ale' 5% brewed under the Greene King label. 'Old Speckled Hen' 4.5%; is brewed under the Morland label and 'Ruddles County' 4.3% brewed under Ruddles label. All their beers although still marketed under the old brewery names are now brewed at Bury St Edmunds.

HUMPTY DUMPTY - Church Road, Reedham, Norfolk, NR13 3TZ.
Tel 01493 701818   Website www.humptydumpty.typepad.com

This brewery, founded in 1998 was originally based at The Railway public house in Reedham but in the autumn of 2000 moved to its present premises. In 2006 it changed hands. The cask range includes, 'Broadland Sunrise' 4.2%; 'Cheltenham Flyer' 4.6%; 'Swallowtail' 4%; 'Humpty Dumpty Ale' 4.1% their flagship best bitter; 'King John' 4.5%; 'Railway Sleeper' 5%; 'Golden Gorse', a strong blond ale 5.4% and 'Humpty Dumpty Porter', 5.4%. If you are travelling in the Reedham area a trip to their Brewery Shop is well worth a visit. As well as selling their own range of beers the shop also sells range of beers from other local breweries plus a selection of bottled continental beers.

ICENI BREWERY - 3 Foulden Road, Ickburgh, Nr Mundford, Norfolk, IP26 5BJ.
Tel 01842 878922   Website www.icenibrewery.co.uk

This Breckland brewery was launched by Brendan Moore in 1995 in the small village of Ickburgh on the edge of Thetford Chase. Their beers are available in a large number of outlets in Norfolk and beyond. The brewery has a large range of beers and has its own bottling plant and bottled beers may be purchased from the brewery shop. Their cask range includes 'Fine Soft Day', 4%; 'Celtic Queen', 4%; 'Raspberry Wheat' 5% and a strong stout, 'Men of Norfolk' 6.2%.

Local Breweries

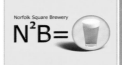

NORFOLK SQUARE BREWERY - Unit 7, Estcourt Road, Great Yarmouth, NR 30 4JQ.
Tel 01493 854484 Website www.norfolksquarebrewery.co.uk
Norfolk Square, from Great Yarmouth, established in 2008 is one of Norfolk's newest breweries. Situated in small industrial unit in the northern suburbs of Yarmouth, this small micro has a range of cask ales that include 'Pi' 3.8% a bitter; 'Scroby' 4.2% a best bitter and 'Stiletto' 4.5% a golden ale. To date the only pub that sells their beers on a regular basis is the nearby Earl of Beaconsfield although their beers have been trialled in The Mariners and Red Herring in Yarmouth as well as some pubs in Norwich. There is also a real ale shop situated above the brewery selling their beers and a large range of bottled conditioned beers from other local East Anglian Brewers.

OULTON ALES LTD - Lake Lothing Brewery, Harbour Road, Oulton Broad, Lowestoft, NR32 3LZ.
Tel 01502 587905 Website www.oultonales.co.uk
Oulton Ales is another brewery from the Lowestoft area. This micro has three pubs and supplies to around 20 other pubs, some of which are in the Yarmouth area.
Their beers include, 'Bedazzelled' 4%; 'Sunrise' 4%; 'Nautilus' 4.2% and a strong 5% bitter 'Gone Fishing'.

REEPHAM BREWERY - Unit 1, Collers Way, Reepham, Norfolk NR10 4SW. Tel 01603 871091
The Reepham Brewery founded by owner Ted Willems has been brewing here since 1983. He, along with Woodforde's, was during the early 1980's one of the pioneers of the new generation of real ale brewers in Norfolk that helped to see off Watneys "Red Revolution". Sadly, Reepham beers are very hard to find in pubs nowadays. The range includes 'Rapier Pale Ale' 4.2%; 'Velvet Stout' 4.5%; 'Tyne Brown' 4.6% and St Agnes, a pale beer at 4.6%.

SPECTRUM BREWERY - Unit 11, Wellington Road, Tharston, Norwich, NR15 2PE.
Website www.spectrumbrewery.co.uk
Owned by Andy Mitchell, a former chairman of Norwich & Norfolk CAMRA first established his brewery in 2002 sharing with Pete Turner's Blue Moon Brewery at The Cock Inn in Barford. Since 2007 Andy Mitchell has moved to his own site in an industrial unit in the outskirts of Long Stratton. Recently the brewery gained the organic certification for all its beers. The beers are mostly supplied to local pubs but some goes to wholesalers and he also supplies some bottled conditioned beer to local beer shops and various farmers markets. The beer range includes "Light Fantastic" at 3.7%, a refreshing beer with citrus notes; "Bezants", 4%, another light beer but with more maltiness; "42" 4.2%; "Dark Fantastic" 3.8%, a dark red malty brew; "Black Buffle", 4.5%; "Old Stoatwobbler" 6%, a very heavy black brew and "Trip Hazard" 6.5%, a very heavy malty brew.

TINDALL - Tindall Ales Brewery, Toad Lane, Seething, Norfolk, NR35 2EQ. Tel 01508 483844
This brewery was established in 1998 and brew mainly bottled conditioned beers.

Local Breweries

TIPPLES BREWERY - Unit 6, Damgate Lane Industrial Estate, Acle, Norwich, NR13 3DJ.
Tel 01493 741007   Website www.tipplesbrewery.com
Established in 2004 by Jason Tipple the brewery now has a capacity of about 6 barrels. These beers
are fairly widely available in many of the pubs around Norwich and Norfolk. The main cask beers
are 'Longshore' 3.6%; 'Ginger' 3.8%; 'Hanged Monk' 3.8% a dark mild; 'Lady Evelyn', 4.1% a light
pale ale with citrus notes; 'Redhead Bitter', 4.2;, 'Lady Hamilton' 4.2% and Jacks' Revenge', 5.8% a
strong dark beer. The brewery has recently opened a shop on Elm Hill in Norwich where all these
beers plus a few more can be purchased bottle conditioned.

UNCLE STUARTS - Uncle Stuarts Brewery, Antoma, Pack Lane, Lingwood, Norwich, NR13 4PD.
Tel 01603 211833   Website www.littlebeershop.co.uk
This brewery was established in 2002 selling mainly bottled conditioned beers. Some can now be
purchased in nine gallon casks. The main outlet is at The Little Beer Shop 58 Yarmouth Road in
Blofield. When travelling in the Blofield area this shop is worth a visit as in addition to Uncle Stuart's
beers a large range of beers from other local brewers is available.

WHY NOT - Why Not Brewery, 17 Cavalier Close, Thorpe St Andrew, Norwich, NR7 0TE.
Tel 01603 300786   Website www.whynotbrewery.co.uk
Opened in 2006 using equipment from Iceni Brewery. Most of their beers can be purchased as
bottled cask conditioned ales.

WINTER'S BREWERY - 8 Keelan Close, Norwich, NR6 6QZ.
Tel 01603 787820   Website www.wintersbrewery.com
This brewery was founded by Dave Winter formerly of Woodforde's Brewery in 2001. It supplies
to a small number of outlets in and around Norwich including The Duke of Connaught as featured
in Norwich Pub Walk 4. Cask ales brewed include 'Mild' 3.6%; 'Bitter' 3.8%; 'Golden' 4.1%; 'Winter's
Revenge' 4.7%; 'Storm Force', 5.3%; 'Tempest', 6.2% and their most recent beer "From the Ashes"
which was very popular and won second place at Norwich 2008 Beer Festival.

YETMAN'S - Yetman's Brewery, Bayfield Farm Barns, Bayfield Brecks, Holt NR25 7DZ.
Tel 07774 809016   Website www.yetmans.net
This brewery was opened in 2005. Their range of beers includes 'Orange' 4.2% 'Red' 3.8%; 'Stout'
4.2% and 'Green' 4.8%. They can be sold in casks or in bottled conditioned form at the brewery
shop, address as above.

An advert to remind us of memories of beers from yesteryear...

ENJOY A
DOUBLE DIAMOND
TODAY

Get outside a Double Diamond and you feel more like

yourself again. A Double Diamond *works wonders*—

takes the tension out of life, revives your confidence,

puts you back on top of your form.

The world is at its best after a Double Diamond.

A DOUBLE DIAMOND *works wonders*

IND COOPE'S DOUBLE DIAMOND BREWED AT BURTON

Useful Websites

Below is a list of websites containing additional information on pubs and public transport that you may find helpful with this guide.

Campaign for Real Ale National Website:-
http://www.camra.org.uk/

Norwich & Norfolk CAMRA branch website:-
http://www.norwichcamra.freeserve.co.uk/

Other local pub websites:-

This site is very good for historical information on Norfolk pubs.
http://www.norfolkpubs.co.uk/

Our CAMRA branch pub site.
www.norwichcamra.org.uk/pubdb

Public Transport Websites

For general public transport enquiries for buses coaches and trains 'Traveline' below may be helpful.
http://www.traveline.org.uk/index.htm

The National Railway website is
http://www.nationalrail.co.uk

Local railway operators:-
www.nationalexpresseastanglia.com
www.eastmidlandstrains.co.uk

For locating places by map:-
http://uk2.multimap.com/

Map of Norfolk
showing Place Locations

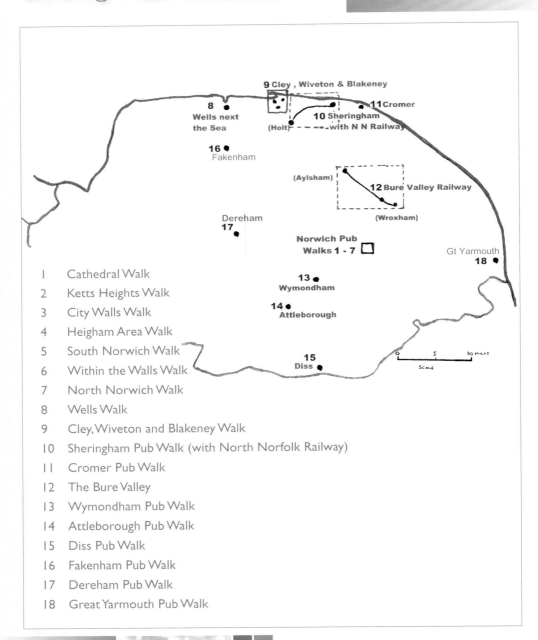

9 Cley , Wiveton & Blakeney

8
Wells next
the Sea

11 Cromer

10 Sheringham
(Holt) - - - - - -with N N Railway

16
Fakenham

(Aylsham)

12 Bure Valley Railway

(Wroxham)

Dereham
17

Norwich Pub
Walks 1 - 7

Gt Yarmouth
18

13
Wymondham

14
Attleborough

15
Diss

0   5   10 miles
SCALE

1   Cathedral Walk

2   Ketts Heights Walk

3   City Walls Walk

4   Heigham Area Walk

5   South Norwich Walk

6   Within the Walls Walk

7   North Norwich Walk

8   Wells Walk

9   Cley, Wiveton and Blakeney Walk

10 Sheringham Pub Walk (with North Norfolk Railway)

11 Cromer Pub Walk

12 The Bure Valley

13 Wymondham Pub Walk

14 Attleborough Pub Walk

15 Diss Pub Walk

16 Fakenham Pub Walk

17 Dereham Pub Walk

18 Great Yarmouth Pub Walk

Cathedral Walk

Introduction

Our first pub walk takes a circular route that starts and ends at Norwich Railway Station. It begins along the banks of the River Wensum and continues to Pulls Ferry and Cow Tower. It takes in the Fye Bridge area, one of the oldest districts of the City that dates back to Late Anglo-Saxon and Viking times. We return with a stroll through Cathedral Close with its many fine 18th Century houses and mews, before reaching the River on our way back to the Station.

We start from Norwich Railway Station and cross over the road at Foundry Bridge traffic lights. Pause whilst crossing the Wensum and examine the cast iron work on the old Victorian bridge equipped with spouts for fire hoses to extract water from the river. On the far right hand side of the bridge is your first pub The Compleat Angler.

The Compleat Angler

This large riverside pub with a terraced garden overlooking the River Wensum was originally built as a tollhouse for the bridge. Later it was converted to a pub by Richard Bullard c1850. First it was called 'The Railway Tavern', later becoming The Norwich Railway House. The pub assumed its present name 'The Compleat Angler' in March 1974, briefly changing to Windsor's in 1983 before reverting back to its present name in 1988. Today it is a popular pub with tourists coming off the hire boats as the first pub most boaters encounter when leaving Norwich Yacht Station. Beers sold here include Woodforde's Wherry, Greene King IPA, Fullers London Pride plus guests.

On leaving the Compleat Angler, take the steps down to the riverbank and continue along the left hand side of the river. You will shortly come to Pull's Ferry, one of Norwich's well-known beauty spots. Pause here to take a look at the old building through

Pull's Ferry

the arch and you will see the beginning of what was once the entrance of a canal that was constructed at the end of the 11th century to convey stones that were imported by ship and barge from Caen in Normandy to build the Cathedral. Pull's Ferry was built in the 15th century and later renovated in Georgian times. It derives its name from a man named James Pull who operated the ferry here in the 19th century. From Pull's Ferry continue along the riverbank to Bishop's Bridge, Norwich's oldest bridge across the River Wensum. On the opposite side of the road is the Red Lion.

The Red Lion

The present day Red Lion was built on the site of an earlier pub dating far back to the 16th century also known as the Red Lion and later The Green Dragon. The present pub was built on the same site, in the 1870s. Like The Compleat Angler, this pub has a beer garden overlooking the River Wensum with views of the medieval Bishops Bridge. A wide range of real ales are available including Adnams Bitter, Deuchars IPA , Fullers London Pride, Shepherd Neame Spitfire, Woodforde's Wherry, plus some guests.

Pick up the path just behind and on the side and continue your walk along the riverbank to Cow Tower, part of the City wall defences strategically built on a bend in the river. This 14th century brick built freestanding structure is the tallest and best-preserved tower of

the city's medieval defences. Follow the river path as it bends until you reach the public car park at St Helen's Wharf and cross to the Adam and Eve in the back right hand corner.

The original pub was built by monks around a Saxon well in 1249 and is claimed to be Norwich's oldest pub. However the present brick and flint building is much more recent, and the interior of the pub

Cow Tower

has undergone many alterations, particularly during the last three and half decades when the interior was completely revamped. Today's pub consists of a series of small bars on split levels serving a range of beers that include Wells Bombardier and Theakstons Old Peculiar. It also offers a large food menu serving meals between 12-7pm daily except on Sundays when lunch is served between 12-2. The pub website is www.adamandevenorwich.co.uk

Adam and Eve

Continue beyond the Adam and Eve along Bishopgate, passing the Law Courts and the church of St Martin's at Palace Plain to the junction with Palace Street. Diagonally opposite in the corner of St Martin's Plain is the Wig and Pen.

Wig and Pen

This pub situated in one corner of St Martin's at Palace Plain, dates to the 16th century and it is reputed to be one of the oldest alehouses in Norwich. The two coats of arms on the front of the house are those of the Broomfield family, well known to Norwich historians. It was previously a Courage House before becoming a freehouse in 1985 changing its name from White Lion to Wig & Pen. The new name derives from the time when the Magistrates Court and Crown Court moved from The Guildhall and Shirehall to its present site close by. The interior of the modern pub consists of one main open planned bar with a small separate dining area at the rear. There is a small beer terrace with tables and chairs at the front of the pub. A large range of real ales is on offer, many of which are supplied by local breweries such as Adnams, Buffys and Wolf plus a number of guests. Good quality food is available both lunch and evenings. More information can be found on the pub's website: www.thewigandpen.com.

CAMPAIGN
FOR
REAL ALE

On leaving, walk down the side of the Wig and Pen into Bedding Lane, and turn left at the bottom and follow the river Quayside to Fye Bridge. On the far side across the road is the Ribs of Beef.

Situated on the banks of the River Wensum and next to Fye Bridge, one of the city centre's favourite locals "The Ribs" is famous for its range of cask ales, local cider, excellent wines and traditional English food sourced locally. It is frequented by local residents, professional clientele, UEA students and tourists who enjoy the relaxed atmosphere, comfortable surroundings and river views. It is also close to the Cathedral and a nearby jetty is popular in the summer attracting visiting boats which moor up to enjoy the pub's facilities. Sportsmen can enjoy live sports on the large screens in the bar. There is a small meeting room available for business and pleasure and hosts various societies and clubs.

The Ribs of Beef

Elm Hill

On leaving the Ribs of Beef turn sharp down a narrow passage way at right hand side of the pub to rejoin the river path which continues along the back of the historic Elm Hill. Turn left through the car park at rear entrance to the City Art College and left again as you emerge into Elm Hill, a picturesque cobbled lane with many timber framed houses. This street was originally an area inhabited by wealthy merchants during the 16th to 18th centuries but degenerated into a slum area in the 19th century. However, after narrowly escaping being demolished in the 1920s the buildings have now been restored to their former glory and Elm Hill is now one of Norwich's most popular tourist attractions.

9 Real Ales
1 Mild always available
Local Cider
Belgian Beers
Big Screen TV

The City's Favourite Local

The Ribs of Beef
Fye Bridge, Norwich
Tel. 01603 619517
www.ribsofbeef.co.uk

When you reach the bottom of Elm Hill cross Wensum Street and the Glasshouse is in front.

The Glasshouse was opened as a new pub by the J D Wetherspoon chain in February 2003. The various public lounges and bars are spread over two floors and there is also a large outside beer terrace on one side. The Elm Lounge on the first floor offers an excellent view of Elm Hill from an alternative aspect. As usual for Wetherspoons, this pub offers a large range of real ales and an extensive food menu serving meals all day at very reasonable prices.

The Glasshouse

Erpingham Gate

After leaving the Glasshouse turn left into Wensum Street and keeping to the left cross over at the pedestrian lights (approximately 200 yards) past the Edith Cavell statue and enter the Cathedral grounds through the imposing Erpingham Gate, built in 1420 by Sir Thomas Erpingham who was the commander of the archers at the battle of Agincourt. In front is the West Gate entrance to Norwich Cathedral. Turn right and cross diagonally over the Upper Close and then bear left into the Lower Close. Continue straight down the slope past some old stables on your left. You are now walking along the course of the old medieval canal mentioned earlier in this walk as you return to Pull's Ferry. Finally turn right along the river and retrace your steps back to the Railway Station.

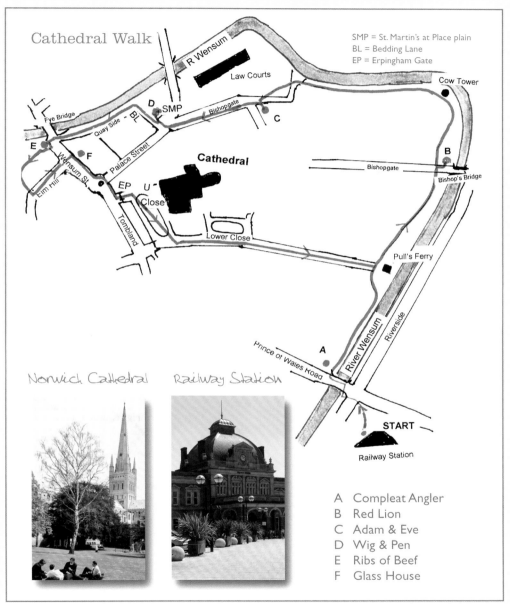

Cathedral Walk

SMP = St. Martin's at Place plain
BL = Bedding Lane
EP = Erpingham Gate

R Wensum

Law Courts

Cow Tower

Fye Bridge

D SMP

Bishopgate

C

Quay Side BL

E

F

Palace Street

Wensum St

Cathedral

Bishopgate

B

Bishop's Bridge

Elm Hill

EP U

Close

Tombland

Lower Close

Pull's Ferry

River Wensum

Riverside

Prince of Wales Road

A

START

Railway Station

Norwich Cathedral   Railway Station

A   Compleat Angler
B   Red Lion
C   Adam & Eve
D   Wig & Pen
E   Ribs of Beef
F   Glass House

Ketts Heights Walk

This second walk, which like the first is circular, also starts and ends at Norwich (Thorpe) Railway Station but takes in a very different part of the city. Instead of heading towards the city centre we head in the opposite direction into the one of Norwich's inner suburbs, the district of Thorpe Hamlet, a largely residential area of mainly Victorian housing. One other big difference compared with the previous walk is that while the first was almost entirely on the flat, this walk takes in short hills that will allow you to enjoy some fine views of the city, particularly if you venture on a short detour to the top of St James's Hill. When starting at the Railway Station (Norwich Thorpe), take a few moments to admire the recently renovated Victorian façade of the station.

The present station was built in 1886 by GER's engineer John Wilson from a design by architect W N Ashby to replace an earlier station built in 1844. The façade is in the style of a French chateau with a centrepiece topped by large zinc coated cupola and two symmetrical long wings flanking each side. Across the road on your left is the new Riverside development of pubs restaurants and nightclubs built on the site of what was once the railway goods sidings and the Boulton & Paul works. Leave the station and turn hard right and proceed along Thorpe Road and up the hill for approximately 300 metres when you will reach The Coach & Horses, on the left, our first stop.

Originally built at the beginning of the 19th century, this building became a pub in the 1830s known as "The Yarmouth Coach". It was first owned by Youngs & Co, then Bullards, and Watneys and closed in 1989. It reopened in 1993 complete with its own brewery, "The Chalk Hill Brewery", which is situated at the rear. Chalk Hill beers have gained quite a reputation over the years winning several awards at the Norwich Beer Festival. The brewing vessels can be seen from a small window along the right hand wall at the Rosary Road entrance. As well as Chalk Hill beers many guest ales are available. For more information consult the pub's website - www.thecoachthorperoad.co.uk

The Coach & Horses

After your first refreshment, leave by the rear entrance and turn right and walk along Rosary Road. After some 100 metres you will come to a track leading to The Rosary Cemetery, England's first non-denominational cemetery founded in1821 by Thomas Drummond. Take

The Rosary Cemetery

a walk around the maze of paths that wind up and down the side of a hill. You will observe many styles of monuments including Classical, Gothic and late Georgian. The graves include many once notable citizens - ex mayors, magistrates, men high in their professions and so on.

On leaving the cemetery, retrace your steps and pass the rear of the Coach and Horses and follow Rosary Road. About 300 metres further on you will find The Rosary Tavern on the right hand side.

The Rosary was built in the mid 19th century and was previously owned by Bullards, Watneys and Courage before finally becoming a freehouse in 1982. The present building is a small friendly one bar pub with dartboard and a bar billiards table. It stocks a wide range of real ales including Black Sheer Best Bitter, Deuchars IPA, Wolf Straw Dog plus guests. Kingfisher real cider is also available. At the rear of the pub there is a small garden with a large conservatory that can be used as a function room.

The Rosary Tavern

After leaving the Rosary Tavern turn right along Rosary Road to the junction with St Leonard's Road and then turn right, and walk up the hill. As you turn, glance back down Rosary Road and you will see the entrance to Bertram Books that stands on the sight of The Nest, the former home ground of Norwich City Football Club. The club moved to The Nest from their first ground at Newmarket Road in 1908 finally leaving there in 1936 when the club won promotion to the then Second Division and the Nest was deemed unsafe. With anticipated bigger crowds the club moved to their present ground at Carrow Road. Continue a short walk uphill and you will reach The Jubilee. (By this point you will have become aware that Norfolk is not all flat).

The Jubilee

This is a typical late Victorian corner pub built in the late 1880s, situated on corner of St Leonards Road and Florence Road. When entering through the main entrance spare a moment and glance above at the relief portrait of Queen Victoria above the door. The Jubilee was originally a Bullards pub before becoming Watneys and then Courage and then a freehouse in 1982 when its name briefly changed to "The Hanover House" until reverting to its previous name in 1986. Today it has a large interior split into several drinking areas and at the back there is a large conservatory overlooking a fine garden. There is a games room upstairs. There is a large range of real ales available which always includes at least one dark mild.

On leaving the Jubilee continue up the hill along Quebec Road for about 200 metres, and you will arrive at William IV on your right hand side.

The William IV was built on the site of a shepherds hut in 1839 and has a lovely brick and flint exterior. Then it was known as the "William IV Tea Rooms". Situated at the top end of Quebec Road, this pub is located at one of the highest points in Norwich with fine views over the city from the garden. The interior consists of one large L-shaped bar with a pool table at one end. On sale is a range of real ales including Adnams plus guests.

The William IV

On leaving the King William, cross into Quebec Road and continue uphill. When the road levels out at the junction with Ketts Hill, turn right (heading out of the city) and proceed along Plumstead Road for about 300 metres. Set well back and standing in the shadow of Norwich Prison and on the corner of Knox Road is The Windmill.

The Windmill

The Windmill was built in the late 19th century and extended in 1922. There is a large car park at the front of the pub where there had previously been allotments. The interior consists of a large public bar with the addition of a long lounge on the Knox Road side. Real ales sold here come from Greene King and include XX Mild, IPA and Abbot.

After leaving The Windmill, retrace your steps along Plumstead Road in the direction of the city centre until you reach the junction with Britannia Road. Here you have a choice of two routes
1. You can continue straight down Kett's Hill to the Ketts Tavern, the last pub on our walk or,
2. If you wish to walk further, it will be worthwhile to turn right and walk along Britannia Road, past the terraced houses. Then on your left there is an unobstructed and arguably the finest panoramic view of Norwich. Turn left and follow a well-worn path across some grassland to a viewpoint where you will find a large brass plaque showing a relief map of city landmarks.

View from Ketts Hill

This vantage point overlooking the city of Norwich is where Robert Kett and his army assembled on 1st August 1549 before storming the City Gates and occupying Norwich. This was time when there was much discontentment among local farmers about the imposition of enclosure laws and Robert Kett of Wymondham, a small landowner, rallied an army estimated at 16,000 made up of local farmers and farm workers. Thus this site became known as Kett's Hill. To continue the story, the authorities in London reacted and despatched John Dudley, Earl of Warwick with an army of 13,000 professional troops to quell the rebellion. After fierce street-to-street fighting the rebels were expelled from the City and finally, on 27 August, at the battle of Dussindale, a short distance from Norwich, Robert Kett was defeated and captured. He was later tried and found guilty of treason and hung in Norwich, in December 1549. His memory lives on, and he is regarded as a Norfolk folk hero.

To reach the last pub on the walk retrace your steps back along Britannia Road, turn right at the T junction with Ketts Hill, walk down Ketts Hill to Ketts Tavern (N & N CAMRA pub of the year 2002) that is near the foot of the hill on your right.

Ketts Tavern

This is yet another pub that dates back to around the 1830s and was originally a Youngs & Co establishment, then Bullards and then Watneys who closed it down in 1976 At the end of the decade it reopened again as a freehouse under the name of "Old Bill", its name derived from the presence of a nearby police station. Today the interior of the pub consists of a large open planned lounge on split-levels with a conservatory at the rear and a spacious beer garden. It has a large car park. An excellent range of real ales are available many of which come from local breweries and include Wolf Coyote, Woodforde's Wherry and Nog Iceni Grand day Out as well as beers from further a field like Hopback Summer Lighting, Nethergate Old Growler, Tim Taylors Landlord and several guests. Home cooked food is available lunch and evenings and meals may be brought in from the nearby Indian Takeaway.

To return to your starting point turn right out of Ketts Tavern and then at the roundabout bear left along Bishopbridge Road and continue along Riverside with the River Wensum on your right. On your way you will pass Bishop's Bridge and Pull's Ferry and at the end of the road you will see Thorpe Station and you will have completed the circuit.

Ketts Heights Walk

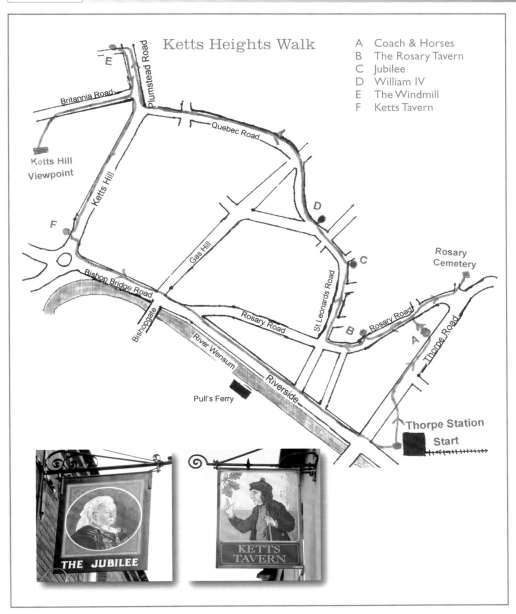

A Coach & Horses
B The Rosary Tavern
C Jubilee
D William IV
E The Windmill
F Ketts Tavern

Plumstead Road
Britannia Road
Ketts Hill Viewpoint
Ketts Hill
Quebec Road
Gas Hill
Bishop Bridge Road
Bishopgate
River Wensum
Rosary Road
Riverside
St Leonards Road
Pull's Ferry
Rosary Cemetery
Thorpe Road
Thorpe Station
Start

THE JUBILEE

KETTS TAVERN

City Walls Walk

Railway Station

This pub walk is a circular tour starting and finishing at Norwich Thorpe Station. The route follows, as far as possible, the medieval city walls that once circled the city. The area enclosed by the city walls was the largest in England, (including London), covering an area of more than one square mile. The walls were built between c1280 and c1340s with 12 gatehouses and 40 towers. The main part of the wall formed an arc round the south and west of the city, from Carrow Hill to the north end of Barn Road, a distance of approximately 2 miles. A small section to north of the Wensum once existed but has now all but disappeared. The River Wensum, a natural defensive barrier, completes the circuit. Parts of the original wall can be seen today including some of the towers. Sadly none of the gatehouses exist. They were demolished between 1791-1808 when the city's population increased and houses were built outside the area of the city walls.

On leaving the station turn right and cross the road at the traffic lights, and walk along Riverside. This part of the walk passes the Norwich Yacht Station and follows the River Wensum. There were no walls built here as the River Wensum was considered a natural barrier. You will note Pull's Ferry on the opposite bank, (For further description see "Cathedral Walk" guide). Continue past Bishop's Bridge, the oldest city bridge, which once had a gatehouse, situated on the city side of the bank.

When you reach the roundabout, turn left, and proceed along Barrack Street. On the far bank is Cow Tower which once commanded the approach to the River Wensum, while on the right is the site of what was once the Cavalry Barracks. A little further on you will pass where the Pockthorpe Brewery once stood home of the long closed Steward & Patteson's, which was taken over by Watney's in 1960s. Little remains of either of these today. On the left is an old mill which until recently was part of Jarrold's printing works.

Turn right up Silver Road, and after about a hundred yards you will reach the first pub on this walk, The Cottage.

This pub which dates to the early 1800s was originally a Young, Crawshay & Youngs pub, then Bullards and Watney. Today it is a typical cosy one bar town local with a large TV screen for live sports. There is a beer garden at the rear. The pub hosts occasional live music. There is usually a range of about three cask beers available.

The Cottage

On finishing your drink at The Cottage, retrace your steps down Silver Road and turn right into Barrack Street. On your right notice a tower and flint wall. This is the remains of Pockthorpe Gate and the start of the northern section of the walls.

At this point the city walls took a northerly direction following roughly the course of present day Bull Close Road. (Here the route deviates slightly from the course of the walls and follows the new inner ring road built in 1969). Cross the roundabout and continue straight taking the footpath to the left of the Magdalen Street flyover. Cross Magdalen Street and continue along the inner ring road. You will then come to another roundabout. Cross here and continue along St Crispin's Road then turn left into Oak Street and The White Lion your next pub is just across the road.

The White Lion

This pub which dates from the early 19th century became one of Norwich's premier real ale houses in 1982 when Colin Keatley (who now owns The Fat Cat) became the pub's landlord. He left In 1989 but the pub's reputation as a fine real ale house continued into 1990s when it was renamed The Tap & Spile. Sadly, in the late 1990s it declined and eventually closed in 2005. Fortunately it has now been purchased by Milton Brewery of Cambridge and reopened in September 2008 selling a range of Milton ales plus some guests.

When leaving The White Lion retrace your steps back to St Crispin's then turn left. Just before crossing the River Wensum take time to look at the fully restored but sadly non-functional listed urinal. Turn left at the roundabout and continue down Barn Road. Here the route rejoins the course of the city walls at the start of the southern section by the site of Heigham Gate.

Walk the full length of Barn Road to the busy traffic lights at the foot of Grapes Hill. This is the site of another gatehouse, St Benedict's Gate, which served as the western entrance to Norwich. Turn right at the lights and the cross to the far side of Dereham Road. Walk a few yards along Dereham Road and the third pub, The Reindeer, is immediately on your left.

The Reindeer pub was built in the 1850s. It closed in 1980 but reopened in 1983 and was the home of Wolf Witham's "Wolf Brewery" between 1985-1995 when beer was brewed on site. The pub was later sold to the Firkin chain and became 'The Finnesco & Firkin' until 2004 when Elgoods moved in and reverted its name to 'The Reindeer. Today it is a one bar pub with a large cavernous interior complete with large TV screens for live sporting events. It stocks the full range of Elgoods beers plus a wide range of guests.

The Reindeer

Upon leaving, rejoin the junction and immediately behind the Public Toilets continue up Wellington Lane which runs parallel to Grapes Hill. On the grass the route of the wall is marked in stone. Walk up Wellington Lane as far as the junction with Pottergate, then turn left and walk to a crossroads where you will see the next pub on the route The Micawbers immediately in front of you.

The Micawbers

The Micawbers dates back to the late 18th century when the pub was called 'The Duke of York'. In the mid 19th century it was renamed 'The Alma', which was retained until 1977 when it assumed its present name of The Micawbers. For a short period between 1995-2000 it became an Irish theme pub called "Seamus O'Rourke's, but reverted back to "The Micawbers" in 2000. Inside it is a large open planned pub with various drinking area on split-levels. There is a good choice of real ales available.

When leaving The Micawbers, walk up Cow Hill until you come to the junction with St Giles Street and Bethel Street. Walk along Bethel Street; take the first right into Little Bethel Street and at the end of the street cross over into and walk along Chapelfield East. On your left is the new "Chapelfield Mall", which was once the site of the former Rowntree Mackintosh confectionery factory. On your right is Chapelfield Gardens that has been a recreation park since 1880. Prior to that date it was a practice area for longbowmen in 15th century, some of whom fought at the battle of Agincourt. In 1666 it was used as a mass grave for plague victims and in 1792 the Norwich Water Board built a reservoir on the site. You will eventually emerge on to Chapelfield Road, part of the inner ring road, when you will be reunited with the course of the city walls. Cross Chapelfield Road via the pelican crossing, turn left for about 200 yards, and you will come to The Champion. Notice as you walk along the road the sections of the city walls on the city side of Chapelfield Road which were exposed in the late 1960s when many houses were demolished during the widening scheme to make way for a dual carriageway. The next four pubs on your route duplicate those on Walk 5, 'The South Norwich Walk'. Only a brief description of these will given. (For a more detailed description please refer to Walk 5).

The Champion

The Champion, now a Bateman's pub is a small two bar friendly town local selling Bateman's, Woodforde's and at least one guest ales. A small range of hot food is available on weekday lunchtimes.

On leaving the Champion turn right. You are now at St Stephen's roundabout, the site of another gatehouse, St Stephen's Gate. Continue right for a few yards and you reach the next pub, The Coachmakers.

The Coachmakers

This pub, once a coaching inn dates back to the 17th century. The interior consists of a bar and a covered courtyard called "The Nedeham Court". Note the large mural on the wall depicting an

St. Stephen's Gate

historic scene of St Stephen's Gate. The beer range includes Greene King, Wolf Golden Jackal, and Woodforde's Wherry.

After your drink, return to St Stephen's roundabout and take the subway across to Queens Road. Part of the city wall can be seen on the city side of the road as you exit the subway. Continue along Queens Road, past the entrance to the Bus Station, to the junction with All Saints Green and Brazengate, the site of another entrance to the city. Continue for about half mile along Queens Road to the junction with Hall Road. Turn right down Hall Road and after about 50 yards and you have the choice of two pubs The Kings Arms and The Freemasons, which are situated opposite one another.

The Kings Arms, the interior comprising of various drinking areas including a large conservatory and outside beer patio is now a Bateman's pub selling in addition to the Bateman's range a very wide variety of guests. It won CAMRA East Anglia Pub of the Year.

The Kings Arms

The Freemasons Arms

The Freemasons Arms originally run by Morgans when it first opened in Victorian times. Until 1994 it was a Courage Pub and between 1994 to November 2004 it was a Woodforde's pub with the name of "The Billy Bluelight". It is now a freehouse selling a range of beers from Winters and Oakham Breweries plus guests.

Retrace your steps to Queens Road, turn right and cross at the pelican crossing and walk to Bracondale. At the beginning of Ber Street was the gatehouse of Berstrete Gates, well illustrated by a large mural on the wall of the Berstrete Gates pub on your left. Once in Bracondale turn down Carrow Hill. Here you have choice. At the top of Carrow Hill is a pathway, which takes you along to the infamous Black Tower, once a prison and then an isolation house during the plague. At the Black Tower a steep pathway will take you down to King Street. Alternatively walk down Carrow Hill and at the bottom, turn left into King Street. On the right, just before you reach Carrow Bridge, was the site of the twin Boom

Towers, located on either side of the River Wensum where a boom across the river controlled access of river craft entering the city. Continue for a few hundred yards and you reach The Ferryboat, situated on the corner of King Street and Rouen Road.

The Ferryboat, situated on the junction of Rouen Road and King Street is another old pub dating back to the early 19th century. It was formerly a Bullards pub, then Watneys and now Greene King. Greene King closed the pub in July 2006. In March 2008 they received planning permission to extensively redevelop the site into a food orientated pub but as yet no work has started on this site. It is not known when redevelopment of the site will commence.

The Ferryboat c 2003

On leaving the Ferryboat turn left and cross the River Wensum over the Novi Sad pedestrian and cycle bridge. Turn left and wander through the new Riverside complex with a variety of pubs, restaurants and bars. If you wish you may stop at Queen of Iceni, a large Wetherspoons pub.

Queen of Iceni

Queen of Iceni formerly known as Lloyds No 1 is a huge Wetherspoons pub, opened in 2001 set amongst the many bars discos and restaurants cinema and bowling alley of the Riverside complex. It has two levels with a capacity for over 2,000 drinkers but despite this it can still get crowded on weekend evenings and at lunchtime Saturdays when Norwich City are playing at home. It stocks a rotating range of real ales, including some from local brewers.

On leaving the Queen of Iceni turn left, walk along the pedestrianised street past many bars restaurants and nightclubs and you will eventually emerge onto Koblenz Avenue where you can cross the street to bring you back to the railway station.

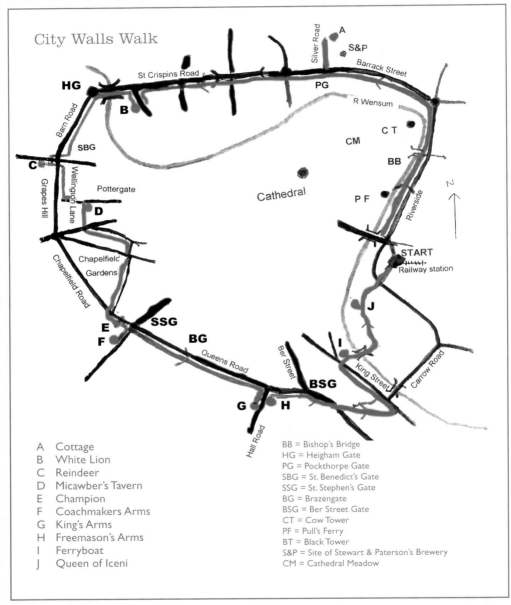

City Walls Walk

A Cottage
B White Lion
C Reindeer
D Micawber's Tavern
E Champion
F Coachmakers Arms
G King's Arms
H Freemason's Arms
I Ferryboat
J Queen of Iceni

BB = Bishop's Bridge
HG = Heigham Gate
PG = Pockthorpe Gate
SBG = St. Benedict's Gate
SSG = St. Stephen's Gate
BG = Brazengate
BSG = Ber Street Gate
CT = Cow Tower
PF = Pull's Ferry
BT = Black Tower
S&P = Site of Stewart & Paterson's Brewery
CM = Cathedral Meadow

Heigham Area Walk

This city pub walk takes you through an area situated immediately to the west of the city centre, just outside the old medieval walls through streets that were built in late Victorian and Edwardian times. The area has had a few pub closures in recent times but still retains a high density of pubs, mostly of the Victorian corner type. There is not time in this walk to visit all of them so our tour is a sample of some of the many pubs in the Dereham Road and Earlham Road area.

Your tour begins at the bottom of Grapes Hill. Walk a short way along Dereham Road leading out of the city, and The Reindeer, the first pub of the walk is just a few yards on your left

The Reindeer

This public house dates back to the 1850s. It was closed in 1980 but reopened as a freehouse in 1983. Between 1985 and 1995 Wolf Witham brewed his own beers on site under the name of "The Wolf Brewery". He later moved to Attleborough to set up his own independent brewery, and the pub was sold to the Firkin chain and became known as the "Finnesco & Firkin". In 2004 after a period of internal refurbishment it was reopened by Elgoods, reverting back to its original name of "The Reindeer" selling a full range of Elgoods beers plus several guests. Today's Reindeer is a large open plan pub with a large TV screen for live sports events. Hot and cold meals are served lunch and evenings.

After concluding your first tipple, begin to walk away from the City along Dereham Road. You will see shops on both sides, but the premises are very different to those which first occupied the street in Victorian times. Gone are most of the baker's, butcher's and grocer's shops which have been replaced by Chinese, Thai, Indian and fast food burger bars. After a distance the shops give way to neat rows of terraced houses, probably the first built along this part of the road. When you arrive at the traffic lights at Old Palace Road turn right. On the corner is a bedroom furniture store which was once "The Dial" public house, originally a Victorian corner pub that was destroyed by bombing during the war and then rebuilt in 1955 but closed as a pub in 1992. The only evidence you can see that this was once a public house is the pubs sign in the car park. Walk along Old Palace Road until you reach a zebra crossing, cross over and turn left into Armes Street Note on the corner a building "Old Palace Medical Centre". This was once a pub called "The Alexandra" that closed in the mid 1990s. Walk along Armes Street for about 200 yards until you reach the intersection with Nelson Street and you arrive at The Nelson, the second pub of this walk. Note opposite a Victorian church with the name "City Christian Centre" with an incongruously added American style church spire.

This pub was originally a Young & Crawshay pub, dating from the 1850s when it was known as "Lord Nelson". Its name was changed to "The Nelson" in 1986. In 2002 Steve Lucas and Roland Coomber (who have now moved to The Kings Head in Magdalen Street), took over

The Nelson

the pub and have made it to a very 'real ale friendly' establishment. The pub is still run by CAMRA enthusiasts and there are regularly about six real ales available that include Caledonian Deuchars IPA, Shepherd Neame Spitfire, Hopback Summer Lighting, Winters Golden and Woodforde's Wherry plus some guests. The interior consists of a small quiet bar at the front and a much larger bar at the back with 'live football TV screen', darts and pool table. It hosts regular folk music sessions. There is a large beer garden at the rear of the pub.

On leaving the Nelson turn left down Nelson Street, a narrow street with terraced houses. You will pass Nelson First School, a typical Victorian structure. Near the end of the street you will arrive at the Fat Cat.

The pub opened in the 1860s under the name of "The New Inn". For much of its history it has remained a typical Victorian corner local run first by Steward & Patteson, Watney, then Courage who sold the pub to Colin Keatley in 1991 who renamed it "The Fat Cat". Since then a great transformation took place and it has become a Mecca for beer drinkers, winning CAMRA National Pub of the Year in 1998 and again in 2004 and is one of only two pubs that has won this award twice. It has a huge range of 25+ real ales served by handpump and gravity, plus 6 Belgian beers on draught, a range of about 30 Belgian bottled beers with real cider also available. There is much memorabilia on the walls of the old brewing days in Norwich when names like Bullards and Steward & Patteson's were the most prominent brewers in the area. For more information consult website www.fatcatpub.co.uk

The Fat Cat

The Fat Cat Public House

- Up to thirty real ales available all year round

- Eighty bottled beers from around the world

- Fifteen continental draught lagers and beers

- Several beers available direct from our own brewery, both bottled and draught

- A varied selection of wines, including fruit wines and mead

- CAMRA's National Pub of the Year 1998 and 2004

- Hand-raised pork pies and filled rolls available at lunchtimes

The Fat Cat Brewery

Brews a fine selection of real ales, including the award-winning Fat Cat Marmalade; together with a variety of seasonal specials.

(01603) 788508

49 West End Street
Norwich NR2 4NA
(01603) 624364

www.fatcatpub.co.uk

On leaving The Fat Cat, continue the short distance along Nelson Street and you will find yourself back on the Dereham Road. Just before then note the fine structure of "Coronation House" with its date of 1902, commerating the coronation of King Edward VII.

Turn right at Dereham Road. Here you will see a very different style of architecture. At this distance from the city, the houses are much larger and grander with decorative front gardens. After about 150 yards turn right into Livingstone Street, another typical street of Victorian terraced houses. At the end of is The Duke of Connaught.

The original pub was built in 1870s but was completely destroyed by enemy action in 1942. The sign was saved and it is still used today. The present pub, a one-storey building with lounge and separate bar, was built in the 1950s. Real ale served here today comes from the local Winter's Brewery, served by both handpump and gravity. This pub is effectively "The Winter's Tap".

The Duke of Connaught

On leaving The Duke of Connaught, retrace your steps back to Dereham Road, cross over and a few yards on your left you come to Helena Road. This is yet another typical road of the period except for a row of new terraced houses on the right. These were built in the 1950s to replace those destroyed by wartime bomb damage. At the top of the rise turn left into Stafford Street where there are views of City Hall, Upper St Giles tower and in the far distance the Cathedral spire can be spotted. Continue down Stafford Street and on the left is Belle Vue, your next pub on the route, with its magnificent Victorian façade.

The Belle Vue

The Belle Vue is yet another Victorian corner local opened by Steward & Patteson's in the 1870s. Also as is common with many buildings in this area of Norwich it suffered severe bomb damage by enemy action during World War II. The interior of the pub today is open planned with a number of different seating areas. Real ales available here include Caledonian Deuchars IPA, Greene King Abbot, Courage Best and Woodforde's Wherry.

Just a short distance further along is "The Chip Shop" well worth a visit if you are feeling hungry. A few yards more and you arrive at The Alexandra Tavern. Notice the pub sign of Queen Alexandra that depicts her face on one side and the back of her head on the reverse side.

The Alexandra

The Alexandra is named after the eldest daughter of King Christian XI of Denmark who later became the Princess of Wales and wife of Edward VII. The landlord "Tiny Little" is known in pub circles for fighting and winning his court battle against Courage over leasing terms in the 1990s. Today it is a small friendly two bar local selling beers from The Chalk Hill Brewery plus a number of guests such as Grain Tamarind, Taylor Landlord and Oakham JHB. High quality food sourced mainly from local produce is available between 12.30-7pm. See website www.alexandratavern.co.uk

On leaving, turn right down Gladstone Street until you enter Earlham Road and then turn left. Underground there are numerous mediaeval tunnels from which lime was excavated which undermine the area. In 1988 there was a sharp reminder when a double decker bus fell into a hole whilst travelling along Earlham Road and spectacular television pictures were shown in news reports all over the world. The magnificent Victorian mansions along this street suggest this was a most affluent area. On the opposite side of the road at the junction with Mill Hill Road is The Black Horse.

Dating back to the early 19th century this pub has formerly been owned Lacons and Whitbred. The interior is on split-levels and it has a low ceiling. There is a separate dining area at the rear and there is a large garden. It has recently undergone refurbishments and is one of the few public houses in Norwich that offers bed & breakfast facilities. A varying range of real ales are available. Meals are available lunch and evenings.

The Black Horse

41

From The Black Horse continue along Earlham Road towards the city and pass the Roman Catholic Cathedral built around the turn of the 20th century. Just past the cathedral you come to the top of Grapes Hill. Here you have a choice. Either walk down Grapes Hill on the left hand side of the road where you will return to the start at the foot of Grapes Hill, or cross the high pedestrian bridge where there are fine views to be had. You may then walk into St Giles Street, which will lead you into Norwich City Centre. Alternatively on crossing the bridge walk down Wellington Lane on the right hand side of Grapes Hill where the city wall once stood and again you will arrive back at the start of the route you reach the bottom of the hill.

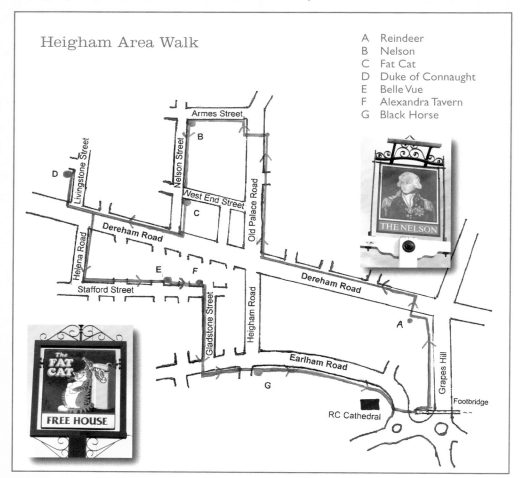

Heigham Area Walk

A   Reindeer
B   Nelson
C   Fat Cat
D   Duke of Connaught
E   Belle Vue
F   Alexandra Tavern
G   Black Horse

South Norwich Walk

We recommend this as a purist's pub walk. It takes in many of the finest pubs that are to the south of the city centre. Of our eight pubs listed no less than four feature in the current (2009) CAMRA Good Beer Guide, and two of them have been voted Norwich & Norfolk CAMRA Branch Pubs of the Year within the last decade. Like other walks, this is circular and never strays far from the old City Wall, starting and finishing at the new bus station that opened in 2005.

From the newly refurbished Bus Station, proceed to Queens Road at the upper end of the bus station and turn right towards St Stephens's roundabout. A short distance in front of you are the remains of the ruins of the medieval City Wall. Descend the steps into the underpass and cross straight over. (You will see a notice 'Samaritans'). Exit at the far end where you turn right and walk up steps and almost immediately ahead is The Champion, the first pub on the walk.

The Champion

This pub, which dates back to the 1830s, was named after a bare-knuckled boxer by the name of Daniel Mendoza, who was a visitor to the area in 1790. The pub has been variously owned by Lacons (as you can see by the "Lacons Falcons" that still exist on the exterior), and by Whitbred, Adnams, and is today a Bateman's pub. It is typical town local. The interior consists of two bars with a small snug at the rear. There is always a wide choice of four regular ales usually two Bateman's and two Woodforde's plus guest ales. Hot food is available lunchtimes only.

On leaving The Champion, turn right towards the underpass and there bear right into St Stephen's Road. You will see The Coachmakers immediately on the right. Note the large mural on the wall above the entrance to the Nedeham Court bar of an historic scene featuring St Stephen's Gate, which was an old gatehouse that defended the main south entrance to the medieval city.

St Stephen's Gate mural

This pub was once a coaching inn and dates back to the 17th century. Nowadays there are four real ales on sale from East Anglian breweries that are served by gravity. In addition to the main bar there is also "The Nedeham Court", a very pleasant covered courtyard set out with tables and chairs. There is also a colourful floral patio at the back. The beer range here includes Greene King IPA and Abbot, Wolf Golden Jackal and Woodforde's Wherry which are all dispensed by gravity.

The Coachmakers

On leaving 'The Coachmakers', turn right and almost opposite you will see the entrance to Victoria Street. You will need to cross the busy St Stephen's Road and you have the choice of either crossing there by taking your life in your hands or walking a short distance further on where there is a pelican crossing. Walk up the narrow and very pleasant Victoria Street with its mainly early 19th century houses and small front gardens to the junction with Grove Road. Turn right and cross at the pelican crossing. Then continue right, cross Southwell Road, and proceed past a line of shops and at the end is The Trafford Arms.

Trafford Arms

Situated on the corner of Trafford Road and Grove Road, the Trafford Arms is a community local attracting a cosmopolitan cliental. It was rebuilt after being destroyed by enemy action during 1942. Since 1993 it has been run by Chris and Glynis Higgins, and they have transformed a once barren Watney's drinking hole into a present day cask heaven. The pub features ten handpumps, including dark mild; permanent beers are Adnams Bitter and Woodforde's Wherry. Real cider comes from Norfolk producer Kingfisher. The Trafford has continuously been awarded Cask Marque since its inception, for consistent beer quality, and has been awarded CAMRA Pub of the Year and local Evening News Pub of the year. It has featured in CAMRA'S Good Beer Guide continuously since 1994. Chris holds a beer festival during Valentine's week, which contributes funds to a local charity. Home cooked food is served all week except Sunday evenings. Best to book first. Website www.traffordarms.co.uk. E-mail mail@traffordarms.co.uk. Tel 01603 628466.

When leaving The Trafford Arms, retrace your steps past the shops and turn right into Southwell Road. Further on you will pass over a bridge that once spanned the railway and led to the terminus at Victoria Station. Although it was closed to passenger traffic in 1915, the line remained open to goods traffic until the late 1980s when it was finally closed to make way for Sainsburys. If you look down on the right you will see the old track bed of the railway that has been converted into a footpath and cycle track known as "The Lakenham Way". It leads to Sandy Lane, just over a mile away, near where once the city line met the main line from Thorpe Station. Having passed the over the bridge, bear left into Trafalgar Street and continue until you reach a T-junction with Hall Road. Turn left to The Kings Arms and immediately opposite is The Freemasons Arms,

Kings Arms

The Kings Arms is yet another drinker's paradise. Like many other pubs on this walk it was originally a Victorian pub and has since been owned by Youngs & Co, Bullard's, Watneys, and Greene King until 1996 when John Craft purchased it as a freehouse and introduced a wide range of real ales. In 1999 the pub won CAMRA East Anglian Pub of the Year. In November 2004 it was taken over by Bateman's who wisely, in addition to the Bateman range, continued the sale of a wide range beers such as Adnams Bitter, Hopback Summer Lighting, Wolf Coyote and a rotating range of guest ales. Inside there are a number of drinking areas on split levels and a conservatory has recently been added to one side of the building, adjacent to a beer patio. A range of lunchtime food is available but you may bring in your own food or food from the local Chinese or fish & chip shop and plates, knives and forks are provided. For more information consult the pub's website is www.kingsarmsnorwich.co.uk

Opposite The King's Arms is The Freemasons Arms. Yet another Victorian Pub, it has had a number of owners including Morgans, Bullards, and Courage and lastly Woodeforde's who took it over in 1994 and completely renovated the interior. They ran a competition to rename it. This was won by Keith Sarsby, a member of the Norwich branch of CAMRA, with his winning entry, "The Billy Bluelight". William Cullum, [1859-1949], alias Billy Bluelight, was famous in the early 20th century for racing down the banks of the River Yare chasing pleasure steamers and selling flowers or other items to passengers. When Woodeforde's sold the pub in late 2004, it became a freehouse and reverted to its original name of "The Freemasons Arms". Real ales on offer here include beers from Winter's, Wolf and many guests.

Freemasons Arms

When leaving The Freemasons Arms, turn right along Hall Road and after a short distance you will reach Queens Road. Turn right and walk past another row of shops until you come to the corner with City Road and The Rose.

The Rose

The Rose began as a shop in 1853 before later becoming a pub in 1856. For a time it was known as "The White Rose". Then in 2002 Adnams sold it to Kevin and Dawn Hopkins. The Rose has now become a freehouse and the interior was completely refurbished and the name has recently changed to "The Rose Independent Freehouse". Like most pubs on this route a wide range of real ales available many of which are from local breweries such as Humpty Dumpty, Tipples, Wolf and Woodeforde's plus many guest ales. Excellent curries from the local Indian takeaway can be ordered from the bar. The pub hosts a number of beer festivals throughout the year.

On leaving the Rose, cross the street diagonally where Ber Street commences. Turn left and continue along Ber Street for about 400 yards and you will come to The Horse & Dray, the next pub of the route.

The Horse & Dray

This pub was known as The Bulls Head until 1938 when it was renamed The Dart Inn until 1977 when the pub closed. It was reopened by Adnams in 1980 who renamed it The Horse & Dray. In July 2006 it underwent temporary closure and reopened again in October 2007. During this period of refurbishment free standing furniture replaced much of the soft furnishings and the pub has now gained wide screen TV for live sports. However, the large patio and beer garden have still been retained. The pub stocks a wide range of Adnams beers including Bitter, Explorer and Broadside and usually at least one guest from another brewery is available. Food is available lunch and early evenings. The pub's website is www.horseanddray.co.uk

You are now on the last leg of the walk. Turn right on leaving The Horse & Dray, retrace your steps back along Ber Street to the fine medieval church of St John de Sepulchre, now a Greek Orthodox Church, and bear right into Finklegate. Cross over where you will see the entrance of Notre Dame School. Then continue to Queens Road and on the right, a short distance ahead, you will reach Surrey Street. Continue along by the wall of the old Convent School and on to The Surrey Tavern, situated on the right hand side of the street and dwarfed by Norwich Union Office buildings. This is the final pub of the walk. A typical two bar Victorian local, it was previously a Bullards, then Watneys, Courage and is now owned by pub chain Spring Inns. The interior was refurbished in 2002. Two real ales are available usually supplied from local breweries such as Wolf and Tindalls. With its city centre location the pub is very popular with local office workers and shoppers particularly at lunchtimes.

The Surrey Tavern

To complete the circuit and return to the start, turn right out of The Surrey Tavern, cross straight over the road at the traffic lights and the Bus station is on the left.

Norfolk Square Brewery

$N^2B=$ 🥛

South Norwich Walk

A   Champion
B   Coachmakers Arms
C   Trafford Arms
D   Kings Arms
E   Freemasons Arms
F   Rose Independant Freehouse
G   Horse & Dray
H   Surrey Tavern

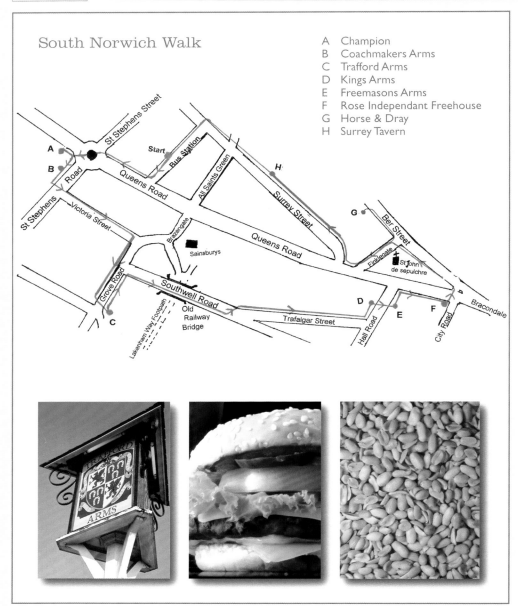

A pub walk around the medieval heart of Norwich. This walk takes you through the heart of the City of Norwich and you will pass through many narrow lanes that were once the streets of the second largest medieval city of England. Not a great deal of the medieval buildings survive apart from many churches, the Castle and the Guildhall but the street patterns for the most part still follow the same routes as they did in medieval Norwich. Many of the buildings you will see today in the City Centre are of Georgian and Victorian architecture and indeed many of the pubs in this walk date back to those times. Their striking facades illustrate the proud boast of "Norwich a fine City".

Our start is in Castle Meadow in the shadow of the Norman Castle whose imposing earth 'motte' or mound was made by the labour of Saxons working (unpaid) for their new masters - Norman overlords. When completed a wooden castle was erected on top to be replaced a century later by the massive stone keep that has changed little over centuries.

Norwich Castle

You begin down the steps leading to Davey Place. At the foot of the steps, walk towards the Market before taking the first right along Castle Street and after a few yards you will see a narrow alley called Old Post Office Court. Just in front of you is the first pub of the route, The Walnut Tree Shades.

This is an old city centre local. The name is allegedly taken from a time in the distant past when walnut trees grew in Gentleman's Walk. The present landlord is a rock and blues enthusiast and piped music is regular! Beers sold here include Fullers London Pride and Wolf beers.

The Walnut Tree Shades

Upon leaving the Walnut Tree Shades turn left and continue down Old Post Office Court and you will emerge on Gentlemans Walk. In front of you is the Market Place that dates back to the Norman Conquest. Immediately behind is the modern City Hall. On the right of the Market you will see a fine old medieval building with a chequer-patterned flint end. This is The Guildhall which was built in the early 1400s and was the seat of the city council for over 500 years until 1938 when the present City Hall was built.

Head towards the Guildhall and pass to the right by the taxi ranks and you will see Tesco Metro. Here you turn right down the very narrow pedestrianised Dove Street. At the end of Dove Street bear left into Pottergate, yet another narrow medieval street. Continue to St John the Maddermarket Church and a few yards beyond you will see the Belgian Monk.

Belgium Monk

This is a recently opened Belgian style restaurant and bar serving Belgian cuisine. There is a very large range of Belgian beers both bottled and draught including some quite rare brews which are difficult to come by this side of the North Sea. There are two floors. The ground floor is mainly a bar although food is served here. The upper floor is a dining area only. There is also a beer garden at the rear.

On leaving The Belgian Monk turn right down an alley under the arch of St John the Maddermarket Church. On your left you will note the Maddermarket Theatre. Continue down and you will arrive at a crossroads and a set of traffic lights. Turn right and close by is The Rumsey Wells, the next pub on the route.

The Rumsey Wells

The Rumsey Wells was previously known as "The Shrub House" and was a previous Lacons and Whitbred house. It closed in the early 80s before reopening on the same site as "Blueberries" and then "Rumsey Wells". (The corner section became a newsagent). It was later refurbished and renamed "The St Andrew's Tavern". This is an Adnams pub selling a large range of Adnams beers plus some guest beers. As of October 2008 it has changed its name back to Rumsey Wells.

You have been passing through what was the work place and trading centre of medieval Norwich whose wealth was largely derived from the wool trade. Red dye was made from the root of the madder plant and was in great demand. Hence came the name of 'Maddermarket'.

On leaving The Rumsey Wells retrace, your steps back some yards to the traffic lights and cross over to Duke Street. Continue along Duke Street and over the bridge of the river Wensum until you reach The Golden Star. This is on the right hand side, on the junction with Colgate.

The Golden Star

The original building can be traced to the 1600s when it was apparently a row of cottages. In the early 20th century it was a Bullards pub and later it was taken over by Watneys who closed it in 1970. Peter Turner reopened it as a brewhouse pub in 1977. Then once more it closed until Greene King bought the property and reopened it in 1984. Today it stocks a range of Greene King beers plus the occasional guest.

Leave the Golden Star, turn left, and walk just a few yards to Muspole Street There on your left is The Woolpack. Notice on the opposite side of the street a large Victorian building that was once one of several shoe factories in Norwich. Now it has now been converted into a complex of modern residential flats and maisonettes.

The Woolpack is a grade II listed building and can be dated far back to the 15th century. It was once a Bullards pub and then a Watneys. It closed in 2001 for extensive internal and external refurbishment, later opening in 2002 as an independent freehouse selling a range of four real ales.

Turn left and continue along Colgate until you arrive at the junction with St Georges Street. Turn right and walk along the now pedestrianised St Georges Street, pass Norwich Playhouse, then cross The River Wensum over the medieval St Georges Bridge. On the far side on your left is the Norwich Art School. Continue and pass St Andrews Hall, venue of our annual beer festival each October and up a slight rise to St Andrews Plain that bends right into Bank Plain. At the end

The Woolpack

of Bank Plain you will emerge on to a large and busy road junction. Cross straight over into Market Avenue. On the left you will note a large Victorian building, once the Norwich Corn Exchange, now the headquarters of Anglia Television.

Continue your walk along Market Avenue and pass the Shirehall that was once Norwich Crown Court and is now the Royal Norfolk Regimental Museum. You may become aware that you are back in the shadow of the Castle mound. Continue along Market Avenue that bends slightly to the left and cross over to the rear of Anglia TV studios. You will then have reached Rose Avenue. Hard left you will see The Steam Packet.

The pub was built in the 1830s. Later in the 1900s it was known as "The Market Tavern" and in 1993 it became "The Steam Packet". The interior comprises of a small cosy triangular shaped bar with a snug at the rear. In 1996 it was purchased by Adnams but unfortunately it is closed at present and is for sale. Hopefully there will be a buyer and it will reopen in the future.

The Steam Packet

Continue up the hill and bear to the left up a fairly steep incline which is Cattle Market Street. On your right is The Castle Mall. Until the early 1960s this was the site of the busy Norwich livestock market and after it was relocated it was a car park. Then, in the early 1990s, a shopping mall was built. From the attractive landscaped gardens above the mall there are panoramic views of the city. When you reach the top of Cattle Market Street you will see the Eastern Counties Newspapers on your left. On your right is Number 12 the next pub of the walk.

Number 12

This old pub which dates to at least the early part of 19th century was known as The Plough until 1973 when it was renamed Le Rouen. In 1993 it closed because the building of The Castle Mall may have undermined the foundations. It reopened again in 2000 as La Rouen before undergoing another name change to Number 12 in 2008. The pub sells Adnams Bitter and Explorer. There is an extensive menu serving both bar and full restaurant meals most lunches and evenings.

On leaving Number 12 continue your walk along Golden Ball Street until you reach the small St Johns Church where you turn right down the narrow pedestrianised Timber Hill Street. Near the foot and on your right is the double named Murderers and Gardeners Arms.

Murderers & Gardeners Arms

The pub dates back to the 1860s when Bullards first owned it. Then later, it became a Watneys pub until it was closed in 1970. After refurbishment it reopened in 1978 as a freehouse with the somewhat odd double name of "The Gardener's Arms" and "The Murderers". Then in 1991 the pub expanded to incorporate the adjacent shop called "The Murderers Cafe Bar" An inspection of the pub sign reveals "The Murderers" on one side and the "Gardeners Arms" on the other. Opinions vary about the origins of the Murderers name. The popular story is that a foul murder was committed nearby but the evidence is dubious.

Leave the Murderers/Gardeners, and continue downhill and then immediately right you arrive at Orford Street and the top entrance to The Bell.

The Bell dates from the 15th century and was once one of the largest coaching Inns in Norwich. It has been a pub and hotel from the 1760s onwards and during the Second World War it became famous as the drinking place of RAF fighter pilots stationed at Coltishall. The pub closed in the 1960s and then reopened as a freehouse until closed again in 1989. More recently, in 1994, it was reopened when Wetherspoons made their first appearance in Norwich. The pub may be entered at either of two levels. The upper floor entrance is on Orford Street and the bottom floor entrance is on Castle Meadow. Also on the ground floor is The Abbey National Building Society. As with most Wetherspoons this pub sells a large range of real ales and and food is available lunch and evenings.

The Bell Hotel

Leave The Bell by the bottom floor entrance, turn right and you have now completed the circuit and back in Castle Meadow having returned to the start of the route.

There is a saying that in Victorian times the City of Norwich had a church for every Sunday of the year and a pub for every day of the year. Our pub walk has taken in a mere handful of the City Centre pubs and you will have passed others. We offer apologies to those that were omitted but reflect that after all you can have too much of a good thing!

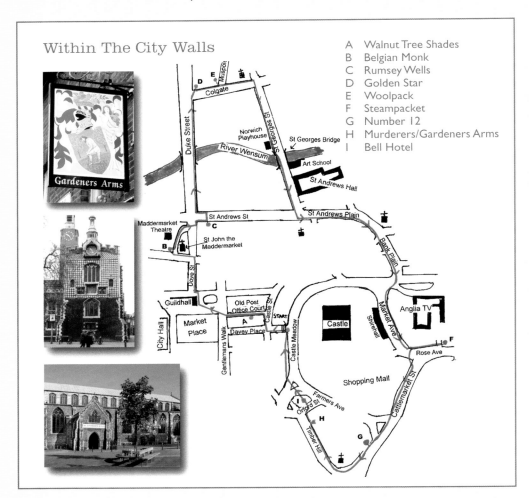

Within The City Walls

A   Walnut Tree Shades
B   Belgian Monk
C   Rumsey Wells
D   Golden Star
E   Woolpack
F   Steampacket
G   Number 12
H   Murderers/Gardeners Arms
I   Bell Hotel

CAMPAIGN FOR REAL ALE

North Norwich Walk

The River Wensum at Fye Bridge

This pub walk takes in the best real ale pubs in the northern part of the City centre and the immediate northern suburbs of Norwich. Starting in Tombland close to the centre of Norwich and next to the Cathedral, the walk crosses over The River Wensum at Fye Bridge and continues along Magdalen Street, the main north route out of Norwich, finishing in northern suburbs of Norwich. This walk is a linear route and not circular like the previous six Norwich walks and therefore finishes some way from its start point in the City centre.

We begin in Tombland near the Cathedral. The name "Tombland" is confusing. It has nothing to do with graveyards but is derived from the Scandinavian word "tom" which means empty or open space. Tombland was Norwich's original Anglo-Scandinavian market place. After the Norman Conquest it was relocated to its present place between the City Hall and Gentleman's Walk. Have a look round and leave Tombland and head northwards. The Maids Head Hotel is in front of you. The first pub Take 5 is immediately to your left.

Take 5

Take 5 is a Grade II listed pub with a timber framed façade that was originally called The Waggon & Horses. In 1976 it was renamed "The Louis Marchesi" after the famous founding member of The Round Table movement. In 2004 it underwent refurbishment and took its present name, "Take 5", and assumed the very different atmosphere and flavour of a continental bar. The pub also has a cellar crypt which can be hired out for private functions and an upstairs gallery where local artists display their work. Real ales on offer here include Woodforde's Wherry, Tim Taylor Landlord and St Peter's Organic ale. The pub also sells real cider from Crones.

After leaving Take 5 turn left and walk along Wensum Street towards Fye Bridge. (That is unless you wish to make an extra stop and go into The Maids Head and have a pint of Adnams in their courtyard bar). You will shortly pass the bottom end of Elm Street on your left and Wetherspoons "Glass House" (as featured in Pub Walk One) on your right.

Continue your walk over Fye Bridge and into Magdalen Street. Fye Bridge is the oldest known crossing point of The Wensum with records of a bridge in the 13th century, although the present bridge dates from 1829. After crossing Fye Bridge continue northwards along Magdalen Street. Magdalen Street was traditionally the principal shopping street serving the north of Norwich, but nowadays there are a mixture of charity shops, second hand shops, convenience stores and many "ethnic" food shops selling exotic foods and spices imported from The Middle East, Caribbean, India or the Far East. For those in need of sustenance there are a large number of Indian and other foreign restaurants along this street. After a short walk you will come to The Kings Head, pub number two of the route.

The Kings Head

The King's Head is Norwich's only keg free pub with all beer being cask with the addition of bottle conditioned beers and a selection of continental and foreign bottled beer. It was reopened after a period of refurbishment in 2005 by Jon Smith and Roland Coomber who formerly ran The Nelson. Cask ales are mainly supplied from Norfolk brewers plus a selection of guests from the wider East Anglia area. Real cider from Norfolk Cider Co. is also available. The pub is split in two distinct areas of which the larger rear area houses a popular bar billiards table, one of only three in the city. This pub has won the branch POTY twice in last three years. It has a varied mix of clientele of locals, office workers and CAMRA members.

When leaving The Kings Head, turn left and continue along Magdalen Street, walk under the fly over, then turn right and proceed to walk to Cowgate and The Plasterers Arms, the next pub on your route, is a little way along on the left.

The Plasterers Arms is an old pub that dates from at least the early 19th century. For a time in the early 20th century it was known as The Knackers Arms. In the mid 1970s it became one of the first Norwich pubs to reintroduce real ale and was a Mecca for real ale drinkers in that period when Norwich only had about a dozen real ale pubs. Today it is a quiet locals pub serving a range of Adnams beers plus guests and real cider from Crones. At the time of going to press (Spring 2009) this pub has just been purchased by Scottish & Newcastle Brewery. Therefore the beer range will alter.

The Plasterers Arms

On leaving The Plasters Arms retrace your steps back along Cowgate and return to Magdalen Street. Immediately to your left is Anglia Square, a large concrete built shopping complex dating from the late 1960s Turn right and continue walking until you reach the traffic lights at the major junction of Bull Close Road and Magpie Road. Cross over here into Magdalen Road and continue northwards. Note on your left as you cross the street a few remains of some of Norwich's old mediaeval city wall, remnants of the northern section.

As you enter Magdalen Road you will notice that the character of the area is changed. The old mediaeval walled area of the city with its many commercial premises is replaced by streets of Victorian terraced residential houses. After walking about 300 yards along Magdalen Road you will come to The Stanley, on your right at junction with Knowsley Road.

The Stanley

Architecturally The Stanley is a typical corner local dating back to late 1890s when it first acquired the name of Stanley Arms. Later in the 20th century its name changed to The Stanley. The most imposing feature of the pub is the large poster located above the entrance of Oliver Hardy and Stan Laurel. Very little of the original interior of this Victorian pub remains as it has been converted to make one large bar. The pub has juke box and music can be very loud at times.

When leaving The Stanley turn right and carry straight on and bear left at the next traffic lights. After about 500 yards turn left into Waterloo Road, then follow Waterloo road for around 200 yards and you will arrive at The Duke of Wellington which is on the right hand side.

This pub is one of the city's premier real ale establishments offering a wide selection of over 20 cask ales dispensed either by hand pump or by gravity from a small tap room adjacent the main bar. It is a friendly and welcoming community pub with many nooks and crannies. The pub holds popular folk nights and supports a bowls team which play in the local park. An interesting feature is a red-brick, Second World War Air Raid Shelter, which is accessed via a trap door and down a winding staircase.

The Duke of Wellington

After leaving the Duke of Wellington turn right and retrace your steps along Waterloo Road to the junction with Magdalen Road where you will find The Whalebone, the penultimate pub of the walk on your immediate left. The Whalebone, situated to the south of Sewell Park is a good example of a community local serving a range of around 10 cask ales that often include beers from Adnams, Fullers, Hopback, Oakham and Woodforde's and is Cask Marque Accredited and is included in the 2009 Good Beer Guide. This pub has recently undergone much internal refurbishment and is broken up into a number of drinking areas. The original front bar is connected to an upper level which has been fitted out with soft furnishings. The Lounge and new Conservatory Bar leads to a covered and

The Whalebone

heated terraced area which is very popular and in the summer hosts barbecues. The pub holds an annual Beer Festival in July and supports 3 cricket teams as well as a golf society.

After leaving The Whalebone cross Magdalen Road and proceed along Lawson Road which is opposite. The Cider Shed, the last pub of the walk is at the far end of Lawson Road.

The Cider Shed

Formerly known as The Wherry this pub has recently been purchased by Colin Keetley (of Fat Cat fame) who also established The Fat Cat Brewery on the same site. This pub now offers a wide range of real ales both from The Fat Cat brewery and guests plus some real ciders. The predominant feature is a large solid oak bar top which holds your attention until your eyes wander to a glass panel from which can be seen a well stocked tap room. There is a large stage at one end of the pub which regularly hosts live music events. The pub has two outside seating areas, plus a newly built cycle park at the front. The walls and beams are tastefully adorned with road signs, cuddly gorillas and railway signals! The pub also has a small, car park and runs a unique bookshop/club for the customers.

If after completing the walk you wish to return to the City centre, there is a bus stop outside The Cider Shed. Bus Numbers 21 & 22 offers a frequent service of eight buses per hour Mondays to Saturdays between 10am around 5.30pm and a half hourly service after 6pm until 11pm.

The Whalebone *Freehouse*
Magdalen Road. Norwich NR3 4BA

www.whalebonefreehouse.co.uk

MENU
2008 CAMRA
Good Beer Guide

● ● ● ● ●

Cask Marque
Ten Cask Ales on Tap
Heated Terrace
Conservatory Bar
Sky Sports
Friendly Service
Quality Wines

North Norwich Walk

A Take 5
B Kings Head
C Plasterers Arms
D Stanley
E Duke of Wellington
F Whalebone
G Cider Shed

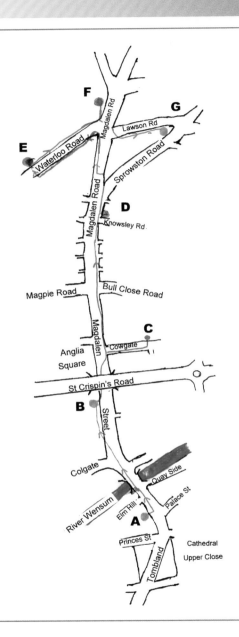

Wells Pub Walk

Wells-next-the-Sea is a small seaside town on the north Norfolk coast midway between Cromer and Hunstanton and about thirty miles north west of Norwich. Despite its name the town is not by the sea but situated about a mile inland and connected by a channel. Although it has the title of a town, many regard Wells as a large village for its resident population is under 3000.

Wells Harbour

The earliest record of Wells dates back to the Doomsday book but by Tudor times it had developed into an important port. Wells continued to prosper and by the mid 19th century it boasted three shipyards where some 60 ships were built. Such was its importance that over 150 ships were registered there. However, after a railway line from Dereham linked the town with the rest of the country in 1857 the port declined and much of the port's trade of coal 'in' and grain 'out' went to the railway companies.

Nowadays, Wells is a quiet tourist resort with attractions particularly for yachtsmen, walkers, and bird watchers while for family visitors there is a superb sandy beach about a mile from the town centre. Something of its grand past remains and although the commercial side of the port is all but a memory there are a few remaining whelk and shrimp boats. The most prominent reminder of Wells of once being a prosperous commercial port is the granary built in 1903 with its large gantry, situated on the quay. This is now converted into luxury flats. A further walk along the quay however will reveal more of old Wells where many other buildings date back centuries and is evidence of the town's industrial maritime past.

Unfortunately Wells is not well served by public transport. The railway link to the town built in 1857 was closed in 1964, and now the only way to reach it by public transport is by bus. There is a "Coast Hopper" service running along the North Norfolk coast between Hunstanton and Sheringham at two hourly intervals between September to end of May and at hourly intervals in the high season, June to August calling in Wells.

Wells Quayside

Sheringham links the National Rail Network via the "Bitten Line" to Norwich. There is also a less frequent bus service between Wells and Fakenham. If coming by car there are a number of car parks the largest being by The Ark Royal Public House on Freeman Street.

The old centre of Wells is small and compact and as the pubs on the walk are within a short distance of one another, it is likely you may wish to make some detours so as take in the full flavour of this delightful small town. Our walk starts at the bus stop on Freeman Street, which is close by the Ark Royal Public House,

Ark Royal

This modern pub dates from the 1960s and was built on the site of a row of 19th century workers cottages. It is a good place to call in before commencing your walk. Situated close to Whinhill Cider works, it has a large car park. Usually a range of around five real ales are available that include Greene King IPA and Abbot, Woodforde's Wherry and John Smiths Cask. If you are hungry, there is also good value for money food available.

On leaving the Ark Royal turn right along Freeman Street in the direction of the Quayside. Those who are energetic may turn left and walk the mile length of the causeway that will bring you to the beach and open sea; a bit of a walk but the views are worth it! Otherwise carry along The Quay where you will find many burger, fish & chip and other fast food outlets as well as amusement arcades. The quay split old Wells into two well-defined areas. The East end of the village was where the landlubbers worked and their chief industry was building ships and loading and unloading the large number of vessels that docked at the quay. The West End was where the sailors lodged. In those days east and west seldom mixed. Shortly you will arrive at The Golden Fleece.

Situated facing the harbour this old pub dates from the late 18th century. On the ground floor there is one main room which is split into two clearly defined areas, a bar with floorboards and wooden chairs and a carpeted lounge area with comfortable chairs. There is a restaurant upstairs. Real Ales available include Adnams Broadside and Greene King IPA.

The Golden Fleece

Before you enter the pub, pause and admire the splendid views across the harbour estuary where numerous boats are moored while further out there are the salt marshes, home to wildlife and many birds. Although the next pub is up the narrow Staithe Street, it is worthwhile to continue a walk along the quay passing under the impressive gantry of the old granary, which will lead you to picturesque old houses of antiquity and narrow alleys leading to yards. You will pass the Chandlers, once a pub called The Royal Standard, and then on to the Old Customs House; and further to The Shipwrights Arms, now a private house but once a pub until 1994, and finally to other ex pubs that once served a thriving community Alas the Norfolk Freeholders and The Jolly Sailor both of which closed about 1904 are no more.

After concluding this short detour, retrace your steps to The Golden Fleece and turn left up the slight incline of the narrow Staithe Street. This narrow street, which is without pavements, consists mainly of old terraced buildings and small shops, an 'olde world' of traditional grocers, green grocers and butchers along with book and antique shops. At the end of Staithe Street is a T-junction. On the left is The Corner House.

The Corner House

This establishment is now a wine bar and restaurant. It was once a pub called the Tewksbury Arms until 1888 and afterwards The Prince of Wales until 1964. It is worth a stop here because although the Corner House is essentially a restaurant three real ales are on tap and you may drink with no obligation to order food, (although the food menu is very good!).

Cross the street and opposite is
The Edinburgh Hotel,

I
This pub is considered as one of the oldest pubs in town and which unusually has the names of the landlords recorded as far back as 1789. The pub is much older than that for its earliest name was The Fighting Cocks until the 1840s after which cock fighting was banned. It was renamed the Leicester Arms until it assumed its modern name. The present pub is long and narrow. The bar is divided into several areas, some plain and others with well padded leather sofas. The main drinking areas are separate from the eating areas, retaining the feel of a proper pub. Beers available include Woodforde's Wherry, Draught Bass plus guest. The pub hosts a popular quiz night on Tuesday evenings.

The Edinburgh Hotel

View of Buttlands

After leaving The Edinburgh, turn sharp left inland into a broad street that leads to a square and a substantial tree-lined open green. This is The Buttlands and the posh end of Wells. Butt means a target and The Buttlands takes its name from the time of Henry VIII when the green was used, (as was law at the time), for men to practise archery. Today many fine Georgian houses and some later Victorian houses surround the open green. There is a choice of two hostelries on The Buttlands. **The first is** The Globe.

Situated at the north end of Buttlands this establishment was originally an 18th century Georgian Coaching Inn. Until recently it was a Greene King pub. After a period of refurbishment this pub now sells a range of beers from Adnams and Woodforde's. The public areas of the pub consist of two bars and a restaurant which offers a wide and varied menu. The pub is very family orientated allowing children into the bar. It also offers Bed & Breakfast accommodation. The pub's website is www.holkham.co.uk/globe.

The Globe Inn

The second at the far end of the green is The Crown Hotel.

The Crown Hotel

This hotel which is situated at the south end of Buttlands was originally a boarding school until the 1830s when it became a hotel. There are bar and restaurant facilities on the ground floor plus a small beer garden at the rear. Here you can enjoy beers from Adnams or from Fox of Heacham. Like its neighbour The Globe this hotel also has an excellent restaurant. For more information on this hotel consult their website www.thecrownhotelwells.co.uk

Finally you have a choice. If you have travelled by bus you can get the return bus at a stop just outside The Buttlands on the corner of Mill Road, or alternatively you may return back down to the harbour to the bus stop outside the Ark Royal. However, if you are still fresh and wish to carry on there is one more pub on the southern outskirts of town on Church Street, The Bowling Green.

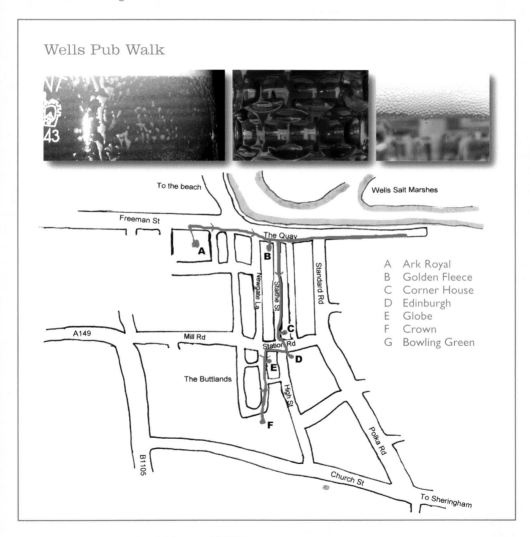

Wells Pub Walk

A   Ark Royal
B   Golden Fleece
C   Corner House
D   Edinburgh
E   Globe
F   Crown
G   Bowling Green

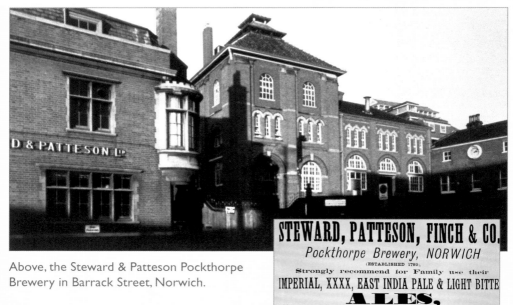

Above, the Steward & Patteson Pockthorpe Brewery in Barrack Street, Norwich.

Right, Steward & Patteson advert c1893.

Below left, the fermenting vessels at Bullards and below right, the boiling copper tanks at Morgans Brewery.

STEWARD, PATTESON, FINCH & CO.

Pockthorpe Brewery, NORWICH

(ESTABLISHED 1793.)

Strongly recommend for Family use their

IMPERIAL, XXXX, EAST INDIA PALE & LIGHT BITTE

ALES,

AND

DOUBLE BROWN STOUT

Which they are prepared to supply in 18 and 9 Gallon Casks.

WINES AND SPIRIT

OF THE FINEST QUALITY.

MANUFACTURERS OF AËRATED WATERS.

CARRIAGE PAID TO ALL STATIONS ON THE GREAT EASTERN RAILWA

Price Lists on Application.

Cley, Wiveton & Blakeney Walk

Forget the City and Market Town Walks! This is as rural as you can get. It is circular tour of about 4 miles in length, along lanes that link the three picturesque villages of Cley next the Sea, Wiveton and Blakeney. City and town dwellers who baulk at the idea of a country walk may choose to cycle or, if all else fails, go by car.

The three villages lie close to the North Sea coast and next to one another. In medieval times all three villages (along with Salthouse, just over a mile to the east of Cley) made up a port around the Glaven estuary known as "Blakeney Haven".

Blakeney Quay

Today what was a medieval port is now fields. It takes some imagination to picture as it was when the estuary stretched as far as Wiveton Church on the west bank and to Newgate Green on the east bank and when at high tide sea going boats could moor up at quays on either side, at Wiveton Parish Church and on the Cley side near the present Holt Road. Then, in the 14th century, "Blakeney Haven " was important as a port for fishing and trade when wool and grain were exported in some quantity.

However, during the 17th century, the port declined as land enclosures caused the estuary to silt up, and gradually by the end of the century "Blakeney Haven" was no more. Land replaced water and Cley and Wiveton became inland villages. Blakeney fared better and continued as a commercial port into the 18th and 19th centuries with imports of coal and exports of grain. In 1780 it is estimated that over 9,000 tons of coal were landed at

St Mary's Wiveton Parish Church

Blakeney Harbour to supply Blakeney, Cley and the local hinterland as far as Holt. Indeed quite large ships were still coming to Blakeney as late as the early 1900s.

In the 20th century, Blakeney developed as a tourist resort and became particularly popular with yachtsmen, ramblers and birdwatchers. Blakeney has great charm. The narrow streets are lined by well-maintained homes of great age. Old port buildings have been converted into flats.

New hotels have been built. The vestige of a small quay has survived where holidaymakers board small boats and at high tide sail the meandering estuary to where the river enters the North Sea at "Blakeney Point". Here there are numerous sandbanks and scores of seals.

There is little in the way of public transport. The only regular service is the "Coast Hopper" which journeys from Sheringham to Hunstanton and passes along the main A149 north Norfolk Coast Road. The winter service (September to May) is two hourly. In summer (July to August) there is an hourly service. The service has a bus stop at Blakeney at the western end of The Quay where it joins the main A149 road, and the other stop is in the main street in Cley. At Blakeney there is a large car park at Blakeney Quay (National Trust). The George in Cley has its own car park and parking is easy at The Three Swallows and Wiveton Bell.

Cley Mill

The walk starts in Cley next the Sea, which is something of a misnomer as it is now about a mile from the sea. The most prominent and best-known landmark in the village is Cley Mill an 18th century windmill, situated to the north on the coast road to Salthouse which was on the old deep water quayside up to the 17th century before the silting of the estuary. It ceased working as a mill after the First World War but was then preserved. Energetic visitors may climb to the top and view panoramic scenes of Cley and the surrounding countryside and marshes. Cley is also renowned internationally as a bird watching site.

The first pub is The George Hotel, situated on a sharp bend on the main A149 coast road.

Formerly known as "The George & Dragon", this old inn of Georgian origins changed hands in 2001 and after extensive internal refurbishment was renamed "the George Hotel". Only the small bar at the entrance is a pub and the rest of the public ground floor space is now given over to dining areas. There are en-suite rooms and self-catering accommodation. Opposite across the road is a large beer garden. Real ales sold here come from Woodforde's and Greene King.

The George Hotel

On leaving The George Hotel turn left along the narrow street, through the pretty village centre of small houses with exteriors of flint with red brick dressings until you reach a bend. Here the main road bends sharp right but your route continues straight on down Holt Road. After half a mile or so, you will reach Newgate Green and The Three Swallows, the second pub of the route. The Parish Church of St Margaret's is situated behind the pub.

With the Parish Church behind and the Village Green in front and with scenic views overlooking the Glaven Valley and Wiveton Church, "The Three Swallows" is the country pub we have all imagined. It was previously owned by Steward & Patteson and Watneys but in 1998 became a freehouse. It has a very cosy interior with two bars, and a separate dining area. The low ceiling, small windows and old fireplaces convey an 'olde world feeling'. The cask ale supplied here comes from Adnams and Greene King. Food is available all day. There is also en-suite accommodation available.

The Three Swallows

After leaving The Three Swallows you may wish to visit the large and impressive St Margaret's Church, which dates back to the 14 century. Its size reflects the prosperity and size of the port at that time in history. When leaving, continue in the same direction as before down the Holt Road. (You may wish to take a short cut across the Green). A short distance will bring you to a crossroads where you turn right to Wiveton. Soon you will come to the 15th century humpbacked "Wiveton Bridge" where you cross the River Glaven. Continue up a short hill and you will reach Wiveton Green. St Mary's Parish Church on your right and The Bell, the next pub on the route, is across the far side of the green. If you think it worthwhile, the St Mary's Wiveton Parish Church is worth a visit.

The Wiveton Bell

The Wiveton Bell beside the Green has a large open planned bar with exposed beams and an inglenook fireplace. There is conservatory at the back, which leads out to a beer garden that in summer months becomes an el-fresco dining area. Beers sold here are from Woodforde's and other guest ales usually from local breweries. Recently this pub has undergone refurbishment and it is now very food orientated.

After leaving The Bell, turn right and take the Blakeney Road that continues into the Wiveton Road and after about a mile you will arrive in the Parish of Blakeney. On your right stands the imposing Parish Church, of St Nicholas. Hopefully you are not tired of visiting churches, for this is a gem and much larger than the other churches. It has two towers. The main tower is very tall with 137 steps to climb to the top, but worthwhile for the splendid panoramic views of Blakeney and nearby villages. The second smaller

St. Nicholas Parish Church

tower on the east side was where beacons were once lit to aid ship navigation which could be seen up to 20 miles out to sea. Today, a light is still lit each evening at dusk.

The Kings Arms

Just past the Church is the junction with the A149 main coast road. Turn left and walk downhill to the crossroads by a bus shelter where you turn right into the old village of Blakeney. Some way along the charming and narrow street, usually cluttered by cars and tourists you will reach The Kings Arms. An attractive white washed flint Grade II listed building with a spacious interior of six separate bars. Five cask beers are usually available from a variety of different breweries served by handpump and gravity. Accommodation is available including guest rooms and self-catering.

On leaving The King's Arms turn left (note the ornate village sign) and down to Blakeney Harbour and The Blakeney Hotel, a large building that dominates the skyline of Blakeney Quay. The Blakeney Hotel is the largest and grandest hotel in the village (AA 3 star rated) with over sixty en-suite rooms. Sir Henri Derterding who was at the time Chairman of The Shell Oil Company, built it in 1923 on the former site of a pub known as "The Crown & Anchor" better known to the locals as the "Barking Dickey". There are numerous public rooms

The Blakeney Hotel

along with lounges including a bar that sells real ale. The hotel even boasts its own indoor swimming pool. The quayside location offers fine views across the estuary and salt marshes.

Leave The Blakeney Hotel, turn right and continue along the Quay. Enjoy the sea breeze and views. You will note a car park where a walk commences that continues past the yachts and boats and across into the marshes. After passing the junction with High Street continue a little further and you will reach The Manor Hotel, another luxury hotel.

The Manor Hotel takes its name from the old Blakeney Manor House. It is a large hotel with many en-suite rooms, and like its neighbour it offers fine views of the Quay and surrounding salt marshes. There is a large bar with a conservatory at one end offering an extensive lunchtime menu. Real ales on sale here are Adnams Bitter and Woodforde's Wherry. Evening meals are served in the restaurant.

The Manor Hotel

When leaving The Manor Hotel retrace your steps to the junction with High street, turn left and you will reach your final pub which is on your right, The White Horse Hotel.

The White Horse Hotel

The original ancient building dates back to the 15th century, but was 'modernised' and largely rebuilt in the 17th century. Today, after more changes it has become a small hotel with a large split-level lounge and a courtyard bar. Real ales sold here are supplied by Adnams.

After leaving The White Horse Hotel turn left and walk up the slope of High Street passing numerous small shops and at the top of the hill you will be back on the A149 main coast road by St Nicholas' Church. Turn left and proceed down the main road back to Cley. After a walk of about a mile and a half you will have returned to the village of Cley and your starting point.

Cley, Wiveton & Blakeney Walk

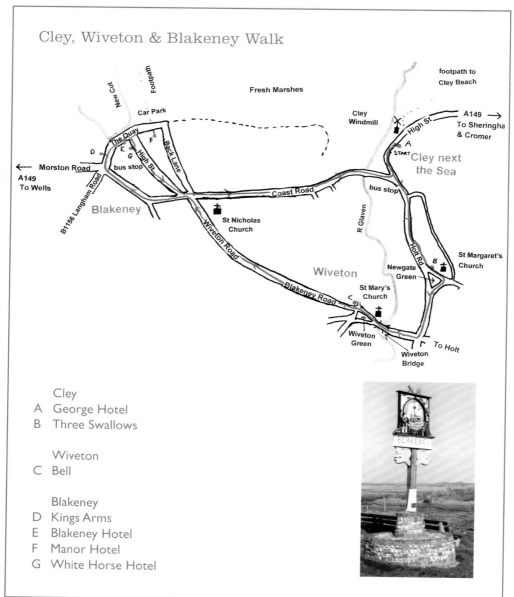

Footpath

New Cut

Fresh Marshes

footpath to
Cley Beach

Car Park

Cley
Windmill

A149 →
To Sheringha
& Cromer

High St

The Quay

START

A

Cley next
the Sea

Morston Road

←
A149
To Wells

D

E
G

F

High St

bus stop

Back Lane

B1156 Langham Road

Blakeney

St Nicholas
Church

Coast Road

bus stop

R Glaven

Wiveton Road

Wiveton

Newgate
Green

B

St Margaret's
Church

Holt Rd

Blakeney Road

St Mary's
Church

C

Wiveton
Green

To Holt

Wiveton
Bridge

Cley
A George Hotel
B Three Swallows

Wiveton
C Bell

Blakeney
D Kings Arms
E Blakeney Hotel
F Manor Hotel
G White Horse Hotel

Sheringham Pub Walk
with North Norfolk Railway

A settlement existed on the top of the Holt-Cromer Ridge as far back as Roman Times. It is recorded in The Doomsday Book as "Silingeham", a name of Scandinavian origin, which translates as 'the home of Scira's people'.

Until Victorian times the main location of Sheringham was on the site of what we now refer to as 'Upper Sheringham' which is about a mile inland from the sea. It was a largely agricultural settlement. In the 14th century a small fishing village began to develop on the present day site of Sheringham and this became known as 'Lower Sheringham'.

During the mid 19th century the fishing village began to expand. By the mid 19th century there were approximately 150 fishing boats operating out of the village. It was about this time that the names were reversed with Sheringham, now a small agricultural village, becoming referred to as 'Upper Sheringham' and the much larger fishing settlement of 'Lower Sheringham' became known simply as Sheringham.

The expansion of Sheringham increased further with the coming of the railways firstly; The Midland & Great Northern line from Melton Constable linking Sheringham with the Midlands which was completed in 1887 and later in 1906 another rail connection was completed when The Norfolk & Suffolk Joint Railway Company built a line from North Walsham via Mundesley and Cromer to Sheringham. This line now linked Sheringham to London via Norwich, making the total journey time from London to Sheringham about three hours. The coming of the railways had a dramatic effect on the character of Sheringham. From a quiet fishing village it developed to become a holiday resort. Between 1880 and 1914 the population of Sheringham trebled.

During the 20th century the tourist resort continued to prosper and the 'fishing village' declined. However, some commercial offshore fishing is still practised.

Today Sheringham, with a resident population of just fewer than 6,000, is one of the most popular tourist resorts of the North Norfolk coast with a bustling shopping centre. Other tourist attractions include The North Norfolk Railway, (which will be referred to later). Behind and inland from Sheringham is the Sheringham Woods (NT) which offer fine walking and rambling opportunities.

Sheringham has railway connections with the National Rail Network via 'The Bitten Line' to Cromer and Norwich and then onwards to London. The other railway link built to Sheringham from the Midlands via Melton Constable was closed in 1964 although a tourist railway, known as "The North Norfolk Railway", and still runs steam trains to Holt throughout the summer season and during holiday periods in winter.

Sheringham
Railway Station

There are also daily bus services via Aylsham and Cromer to and from Norwich as well as "The Coast Hopper Service" which travels along the north Norfolk coast to Hunstanton, and then onwards to King's Lynn. If coming to Sheringham by car there are plenty of car parks, the biggest and most accessible being the one just off the main A149 Cromer Road by the North Norfolk Railway Station.

This walk starts at the crossroads next to the Bittern Line Station. Proceed across the street towards the Tourist Information Office. At the booking hall of The North Norfolk Railway Station, cross the road and pass to the left of St Peter's Church along St Peter's Road until you come to a crossroads and the junction with Church Street. Cross over and proceed along The Boulevard. At the end of The Boulevard you will come to a roundabout which has a war memorial surrounded by an ornate formal garden. This memorial was built in 1921 to commemorate those killed in the First World War and is 26 feet high. Names of those killed in the Second World War were later added. Cross straight over at The Memorial roundabout to The Esplanade. When you reach a T-junction turn right to the end of the street and The Burlington Hotel, the first stop of the route is on your right.

Sheringham
War Memorial

The Burlington Hotel is an imposing Victorian structure of several storeys built in 1899, just after the coming of the railways to Sheringham. It dominates the immediate area. Today it is a hotel with a large bar on the ground floor open to non-residents selling one real ale, which is usually Courage Best Bitter. There are good views of the North Sea from this bar.

On leaving The Burlington Hotel cross the grass in front of the hotel. Walk down a set of steps to the sea front promenade. Turn right. After walking a small distance climb a steep slope to 'Lobster Plain' and walk past the Fisherman's lifeboat and the shingle beach. Continue along the promenade and you will shortly come to the north end of High Street and the second pub, The Two Lifeboats Hotel.

The Two Lifeboats Hotel is a small seafront hotel with commanding views of the North Sea and Sheringham beach from its front windows. A range of Greene King cask beers is sold here. There is an extensive food menu, which includes local dishes such as crab and lobster. There is a beer terrace on the seaward facing side of the pub.

The Two Lifeboats

Further along the promenade you will come to The Crown, the next pub on the route.

The Crown

The Crown, set back from the seafront and like its near neighbour, "The Two Lifeboats", also has commanding views of the beach and North Sea. In fact the pub has had to be rebuilt further back from the seafront two or three times in recent history because of coastal erosion. It has live music on Friday and Sunday evenings. Real ales sold here include Adnams, Charles Wells Bombardier and Woodforde's Wherry. For further information consult website www.crownsheringham.co.uk

When you leave The Crown back track via Gun Street to The High Street and you will now find yourself in the heart of old Sheringham with cafes, souvenir shops and amusement arcades. A few yards to your left is The Lobster.

An old three bar pub situated at the seaward end of the High Street. There is a lively public bar, a comfortable wood panelled lounge and at the rear there are converted stables which now form a modern dining area. Please note that the real ale fonts are all in the lounge area and customers entering via the bar may think this pub has no real ale. The pub sells a wide range of real ales from Adnams, Greene King, Marston's plus many guests. Real cider is also available. Food is available lunch & evenings and all day during the summer season. Check out Website address www.the-lobster.com

The Lobster

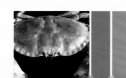

When leaving The Lobster turn left down Wyndham Street and about 100 yards further on you will come to The Windham Arms. Note a plaque on the building on the opposite side of the street stating that the first ever bomb dropped from the air on British soil was from a Zeppelin in 1915 which landed on this building.

Sheringham Preservation Society Plaque

The Windham Arms

The Windham Arms is a comfortable friendly two bar pub, built in the early 19th century with Dutch style gables and flint and white washed walls. There is a large outdoor beer terrace which is popular during summer months. It has a sea view at the far end which is only around 50 yards from the sea front. Real ale sold here comes from Adnams, Woodforde's, Humpty Dumpty plus a number of guest ales. There is a large carpeted lounge bar plus a smaller bar. The pub's food menu specialises in Greek food.

After departing from The Windham Arms, retrace your steps down Wyndham Street and turn left into High Street. Follow down High Street until you come to The Clock Tower, one of Sheringham's best-known landmarks. It was built in 1862 as a reservoir and included both a horse trough and a tap for use by the local residents. The clock on the top of the tower dates back to 1901. Pass the clock tower into Station Road and a short distance on your left is The Robin Hood, the next pub on your route.

The Clock Tower

The Robin Hood

The Robin Hood built in the late 19th century, with a red brick and flint exterior, has recently re-opened after a period of closure. There has been extensive internal refurbishment with white and wooden panelled walls. The flooring is mainly wooden, with a small area that has been carpeted. Real ales on sale here come from Adnams and Greene King.

On leaving The Robin Hood turn left along Station road and you will shortly be back at the start point. You can now either finish your walk, or if you wish to carry on there is The Dunstable Arms, which is about 5 minutes walk down Cromer Road. (See bottom right corner of map). Alternatively you may wish to try some other pubs and take a trip on The North Norfolk Railway.

Black Prince

Weybourne Station

The North Norfolk Railway, also known as "The Poppy Line", goes from Sheringham to Holt, a distance of some five and a half miles. It operates over a small section of what was once "The Midland & Great Northern Railway," of which the Sheringham section of the line (from Melton Constable) was opened in 1887. It closed for passenger traffic in 1964. A preservation society was established shortly after closure and the three-mile section between Sheringham to Weybourne was purchased. In 1976 a Light Railway Order was granted allowing trains to run along this stretch of track. Later the length of the line was extended to Kelling Camp Halt in 1983 and finally passenger traffic was opened as far as Holt in 1989, where the line terminates today. See website www.nnrailway.co.uk

There are no pubs which are close to the line, but there are some if you are prepared to walk a little distance. Alternatively look for the "Gresley Buffet Car" where you can purchase premium-bottled beers on board the train to drink enroute. They also sometimes have cask 'bright' beer on sale as well.

Your journey starts at the ornate Victorian Sheringham Station (see page 73), originally built in 1887 when the railway first came to the town. Very shortly after you leave you will pass through the suburbs of Sheringham and past a golf course. You will soon break out into the open countryside and go over an embankment before crossing over the A149 coast road. On your right hand side are some stunning views of the north Norfolk coast, and on your left is a wooded area known as "Sheringham Park" which is owned by the National Trust. Soon on your right down a hill you will have a distant view of Weybourne village with its distinctive windmill. Weybourne Station is a gem of a rural preserved station which was built in 1900. The present restored building includes the booking hall, a bookshop and a small café and souvenir shop. Adjacent to the station are the sheds where the locomotives, carriages and wagons are maintained and restored.

Weybourne village is over a mile from the station. If you walk down the hill from the station and into the attractive village, situated on the coast, there is The Ship Inn in the village centre. This is well worth a visit. The Weybourne Ship, dates backs to Georgian times but most of the

The Weybourne Ship

present building is Edwardian. Internally it consists of a lounge, a bar & sports room and a restaurant serving a wide range of home cooked food often locally sourced. There is a constantly changing range of real ales available including beers from Woodforde's, Humpty Dumpty and Yetman's, plus guests from other local micros and well-known independent breweries. For more information check out www.shipinnweybourne.co.uk

On leaving Weybourne the route continues through some woods and heathland countryside called Kelling Heath. There is a small platform here (Kelling Camp Halt), but steam trains only stop here by request on the return leg of the journey because of a steep up hill gradient. It is worth getting off here if you wish to ramble around the local woods and heath land. During the final part of your journey the countryside changes to arable fields before you finally arrive at Holt, a journey of some five and a half miles. This station, which is the south western terminus of the line, is the result of a lot of recent building after Stalham Station was painstakingly dismantled, transported and rebuilt here at Holt. In addition there is a brick goods shed which has become a museum and a water tower have also been constructed.

A walk to Holt is just over a mile and passes Gresham's Public School. More recently to relieve passengers an ex-London Routemaster bus has been introduced. In any case a visit to Holt is well worth while to see this small very attractive north Norfolk town. The original settlement of Holt dates back to Saxon times and is mentioned in the Doomsday book. Today the town centre consists of almost entirely Georgian buildings. There are three pubs to choose from in the town centre, which are all close to one another. Firstly,

there is The Railway Tavern, on Station Road. Secondly, The Feathers Hotel, an old coaching inn situated in the centre of the Market Place. Greene King IPA and Abbot are sold here. A little further along the street in The High Street is The Kings Head, another old inn with parts of the

Railway Tavern

Feathers Hotel

The Kings Head

original building dating as far back as the 18th century. This is a local's pub selling a range of Adnams and Woodforde's real ales.

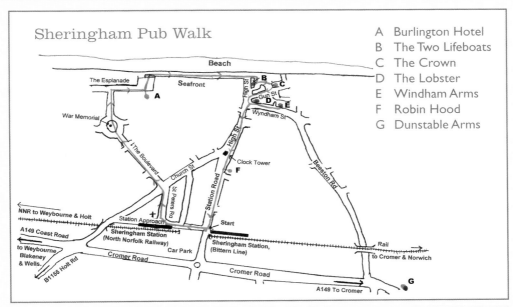

Sheringham Pub Walk

A Burlington Hotel
B The Two Lifeboats
C The Crown
D The Lobster
E Windham Arms
F Robin Hood
G Dunstable Arms

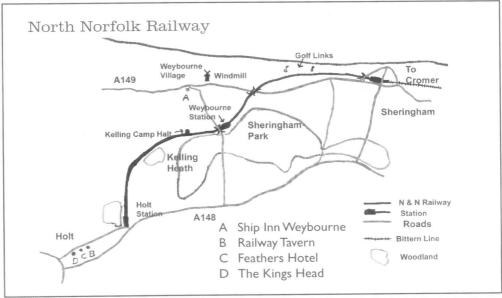

North Norfolk Railway

A Ship Inn Weybourne
B Railway Tavern
C Feathers Hotel
D The Kings Head

N & N Railway
Station
Roads
Bittern Line
Woodland

Cromer Pub Walk

Cromer is a small town perched on a high cliff overlooking and facing the North Sea. Its 13th century name was 'Crowmere' from the old English meaning "a lake frequented by crows". Despite not having a harbour, Cromer has long been a fishing village, and today as in yesteryears, fishing boats can still be seen hauled up on the high beach, overlooked on the cliff top by the medieval layout of twisting narrow streets. However, in the latter part of the 19th century the town expanded when the Great Eastern Railway reached the town in 1877 from Norwich followed by The Midland & Gt Northern Railway from Melton Constable in 1887. This gave Cromer rail links from both the south of England and the

View of Cromer Pier

Midlands. Cromer now boasting a pier became a favourite sea-side resort of the affluent upper middle classes of the day and many sumptuous hotels were built to accommodate them. Something of this flavour still exists today although Cromer is favoured largely by families seeking a quiet holiday away from its larger neighbours such as Great Yarmouth.

The Pub walk starts at Cromer Beach Railway Station. As you leave the platform you will see the first pub The Station House which is immediately in front and slightly to the right.

This was the original Cromer Beach Station, the offices of which closed in 1965 when the station became unmanned. After closure it initially became travel agency until 1998 when it was converted into a pub originally known as Buffers, but more recently it was renamed "Station House". The interior contains much railway memorabilia reminding us of its former days as a station terminal. Today's pub is a Greene King establishment selling IPA Abbot and Old Speckled Hen. Food is served lunch and evenings from 12-3pm and 6-9pm. The pub has a function/conference room.

The Station House

On leaving Buffers turn left and walk down the busy Holt Road towards the town centre and directly in front you will see church tower, which dominates the skyline of Cromer. Crossover a small roundabout into West Street and a few yards on the left hand side you will come to The White Horse.

The Station House

The White Horse is a typical Victorian town local. The interior has two bars, one of which is a games room with pool, darts and a large TV screen for live sports. There is also a heated patio. A range of three real ales are usually available including Charles Wells Bombardier and Adnams. Hot and cold food is served Mon-Sat 12-2.30 and 6-9pm. Sunday lunch is from 12-4pm. This public house also provides bed and breakfast.

From the White Horse continue along West Street, until you reach a somewhat complicated road junction. Cross diagonally and continue on West Street and you will arrive in Church Street, the shopping centre of Cromer. Bear right pass the unmistakeable 'Icarus Hines,' Quality Butcher!

"Icarus Hines"
Quality
Butcher

Continue past the Parish Church, St Peter & St Paul, boasting the tallest church tower in Norfolk at 160 feet. This served as a lighthouse until the first purpose built lighthouse was constructed in 1719. The church is well worth a visit if only to see a memorial to Henry George Blogg G.C. and B.E.M. (1876-1954) who joined the lifeboat crew in 1894 and served 53 years in the Cromer Life-Boats during which time some 873 lives were saved from shipwrecks. Those with an energetic disposition may pay £1 and climb the tower and enjoy magnificent views of the town and North Sea coast. A short distance past the Church turn left down a narrow street (Brook Street), and at the end you will come to The Red Lion Hotel.

Henry Blogg (1876-1954)

WOODFORDE'S
Norfolk Ales

This Victorian cliff top hotel has many ensuite rooms, two bars, one a traditional bar with mahogany panelling and the other a modernised lounge that is flint walled and decorated with photographs depicting Cromer's maritime past. There is usually a choice of four real ales available which normally include Adnams Bitter and Woodforde's Wherry. This hotel has a large restaurant, known as "Galleons" offering an extensive menu.

The Red Lion Hotel

The Pier and Lifeboat Station from the Red Lion Hotel

You are now in the heart of what was once the ancient medieval village. In front of The Red Lion is a cliff top view of the promenade below, with the beach and the pier, (built in 1901), and the pavilion theatre which plays host during the summer season to the very popular 'The End of the Pier Show'. At the far end of the pier is the Cromer Lifeboat Station.

When leaving The Red Lion turn left along Tucker Street and along the rear of the church and then bear right down the narrow High Street past the junction with Jetty Street. Pass the famous Hotel de Paris and a short distance on the left you come to The Kings Head.

The Kings Head

This L-shaped white washed flint building with a lovely headboard depicting Henry VIII dates back to the late 18th or early 19th century. Today it is a busy bustling pub with plenty of atmosphere including a large TV sports screen and a pool table. A small selection of real ales are available that include Adnams Broadside and Woodforde's Wherry. Food is available lunchtime until 5pm.

Close by are the next two pubs enroute, The Wellington Hotel and The Dolphin.

The Wellington

The Wellington Hotel which provides ensuite rooms, dates back to the latter part of the 18th century. Nowadays it is a small hotel with a large long non residents one-room bar downstairs. There are usually about three real ales available including Adnams Bitter, Courage Directors and a house beer called 'Old Welly'.

When you have finished your drink you may cross New Street and enter The Dolphin via the rear door or alternatively proceed to the cliff top and before entering via the main door to your left, enjoy a fine view of Cromer Pier.

"a fine view of Cromer Pier"

The Dolphin also dates back from about the same period as the Wellington. It is on two levels with a restaurant on the upper floor and the bar/lounge with separate games area on the lower. The restaurant is open Monday to Friday 12-2.30 and 6-9pm. On Saturdays and Sundays opening times are from 12-9pm. Great views of Cromer pier can be seen through the windows on the seaward side of the building. In fact it was once called The Cliff Hotel in the late 1890s and has only been known as The Dolphin since 1988. Real ales including beers from Adnams and Woodforde's Wherry are available.

The Dolphin

The last pub is a distance away. Turn right upon leaving The Dolphin and proceed along New Street until you come to the Main Road at the junction of Prince of Wales Road and Runton Road. Cross the main road here and walk along Runton Road with the sea, promenade and gardens on your right. Just past the junction with Cabbell Road you will arrive at the last pub of the walk. The Anglia Court Hotel.

The Anglia Court Hotel

This hotel is situated on Runton Road and enjoys good cliff top views of the North Sea. There is a large non-residents bar on the ground floor. A selection of real ales are available that include beers from Woodforde's and Wolf breweries. The restaurant is open Tuesday to Thursdays 12-2 and 6 to 8pm and on Fridays and Saturdays 12-2 and 6-9pm. No food Sunday and Monday. For more details see hotel website www.angliacourthotel.com

To return to the start of the route (the railway station) turn right on leaving The Anglia Court Hotel, then right again down Cabbell Road until you reach West Street. Turn right and follow the road to the station and you are back at the start and have completed the circuit.

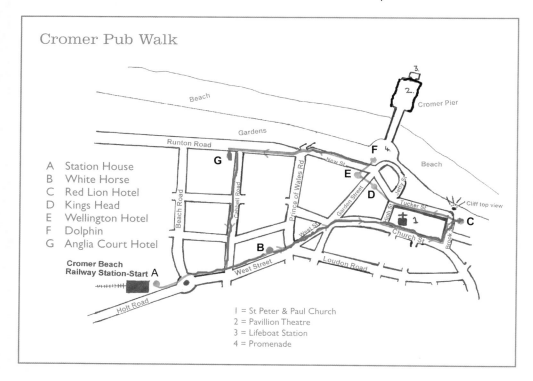

Cromer Pub Walk

A   Station House
B   White Horse
C   Red Lion Hotel
D   Kings Head
E   Wellington Hotel
F   Dolphin
G   Anglia Court Hotel

Cromer Beach
Railway Station-Start A

1 = St Peter & Paul Church
2 = Pavillion Theatre
3 = Lifeboat Station
4 = Promenade

The Bure Valley

The Bure Valley trail is a nine-mile trip from Aylsham to Wroxham. You may walk, cycle or take a more sedate form of travel by riding on the 15" narrow gauge Bure Valley Railway.

In 1987 Broadland District Council acquired the section of track between Aylsham and Wroxham and in 1989 the newly formed "Bure Valley Railway Ltd" took a lease for half of the track bed and started laying the 15" narrow gauge track leaving the other half of the former British Rail track bed to The Broadland District Council who built a permanent footpath and cycle way running parallel with the narrow gauge railway line.

The line opened for business in the summer of 1990 running the full nine-mile length from Aylsham to Wroxham. There are three intermediate stations at Brampton, Buxton and Coltishall where passing loops were built. In March 1991 the footpath was completed and became known as "The Bure Valley Walk". The number of passengers using the line have gradually grown over the years and the railway together with the footpath running along side make it one of north east Norfolk's major tourist attractions.

Today the company owns and maintains a fleet of locos and coaches which are housed at Aylsham. Passenger services run daily from mid March until the end of September, together with 'Santa' Specials' around Christmas and the New Year holidays. For more information consult their website which is www.bvrw.co.uk.

Getting There.
The Wroxham end of the line is less than five minutes walk from Network Rail's "Bittern Line" running from Norwich to Cromer and Sheringham. If travelling from Norwich Station it is possible to purchase a through ticket from Norwich to Aylsham by asking for a "Bure Valley Extension" ticket. There are also regular bus services connecting Norwich with both Aylsham and Wroxham. Aylsham also has bus-connecting services with Cromer and Sheringham and Holt. If travelling by car, there is ample car parking space at both Wroxham and Aylsham, although the car parks particularly at the Aylsham end can become full in high season.

The Route from Aylsham to Wroxham.
Aylsham is a very old Norfolk market town dating back to Anglo Saxon times. It derives its name from a chief named Aegel, and this is Aegel's homestead in old English. Aylsham is recorded in the Domesday Book under the name of "Elesham". The town rose to prominence in common with most local Norfolk towns in later medieval times when it prospered as a result of the linen trade and then later in the 15th century from wool, particularly the weaving of worsted cloth which was a major industry at that period.

BUFFY'S
HOPLEAF

The fortunes of the town declined with the coming of the industrial revolution when textile trade moved to other parts of the country. However, it retained some importance as an agricultural market town as seen by its many fine Georgian buildings particularly around the Market place. A canal was cut alongside the Bure down towards Coltishall in the late 18th century mainly to carry agricultural produce. There was also a turnpike connecting Aylsham with Norwich which opened in 1794 and later extended to Cromer. In the 1880s the railways came to Aylsham further boosting its transport links.

Today Aylsham is a small agriculturally based town with light industry and some tourism. It is close to the Broads and Blickling Hall is nearby.

Aylsham Pubs

The town centre of Aylsham has three pubs, which are close to one another. Our walk starts at the old medieval market place. The town was first granted a charter in 1296 and the market has remained on the same site ever since. The National Trust today owns the site.

Aylsham Market square

First is The Black Boys situated in a commanding location on the west side of the market square. Pause before you enter the pub to see the Victorian town Hall on the north side of the square that was built in the 1850s. You may also catch a glimpse of the impressive medieval St Michael's parish church, (which is well worth a visit).

The Black Boys

The Black Boys, parts of which date back to 1655, is one of the most prominent buildings in the market square and has always been an important meeting place in the town. The exterior is decorated with black boys. It also has a claim to fame that once Admiral Nelson danced here. Today the pub is a small hotel with a large public bar at the front. It offers a wide ranging food menu and real ales from Woodforde's, Adnams and Greene King are usually available.

On leaving The Black Boys turn right and cross Penfold Street into Hungate Street and past the post office to the second pub The Unicorn.

The Unicorn has a splendid red tiled roof and is another old building dating back to the 18th century. Like The Black Boys it also stocks a range of real ales such as John Smith's Marston's Pedigree and Greene King Old Speckled Hen. Food is available at lunchtimes between 12 and 2pm. Its character is more of a back street local with dartboard and other pub games.

The Unicorn

Our third pub is The Feathers, which is situated on Cawston Road. On leaving the Unicorn retrace your steps back to Penfold Street and walk on until you reach the old thatched roofed Pump House where you turn left into Cawston Road and after a short distance on your right you will come to The Feathers.

The Feathers

The Feathers, a flint and brick built Victorian building is a welcoming local's pub. The comfortable main bar has low ceilings and many old Bullard's and Steward & Patteson memorabilia to decorate its walls. There is also another smaller bar. Real Ales on offer here include Charles Wells Bombardier and a frequently changing list of guests which often include local ales from Oulton and Humpty Dumpty Breweries.

It is now time to board the train on The Bure Valley Railway or if you are feeling energetic commence either walking or cycling along "The Bure Valley Walk". The railway station is situated down Blickling Road about a five to ten minute walk from the market square in a southeasterly direction.

The Train Journey

Aylsham station is the headquarters of The Bure Valley railway. If you have time, it well worth looking at the locomotive depot that is open to the public and view the locomotives and rolling stock being maintained and repaired. Take your seat in a diminutive carriage and soon you will pass through a tunnel under the A140 Aylsham by-pass. Thereafter you find yourself riding through the open countryside of the Upper Bure Valley with views of the River Bure on your left. After about two miles you reach the first station, Brampton, a small village without pubs. After about another mile you arrive at the village of Buxton where you may wish to break your journey.

Buxton with Lamas

It is well worth breaking your journey at Buxton Station. The parish of Buxton with Lamas comprises two villages, Buxton on the south side of the River Bure and Lamas to the north of the river. Retrace your steps down the lane back towards Buxton village centre. Once you reach the main road turn right past the impressive village hall and some immaculate playing fields and after a short walk you will reach The Old Crown.

The Old Crown is an old hostelry dating back at least to the early 19th century. It has an imposing Dutch gable at one end. The pub was formerly owned by Steward & Patteson, then a Watneys pub and was closed for a while in 1999 before being re-opened as free house later the same year. The interior is just what you would expect

The Old Crown

of a pub of this age. There is a separate dining area where food is available both lunch and evenings. The pub is open all day Saturdays and Sundays but closes in the afternoon on weekdays. It stocks a range of real ales, which include Adnams.

The next station is Coltishall. It is highly recommended that you make a stop here as, with its neighbouring village Horstead just across the Bure, there are no less than five excellent pubs that are in close proximity to Coltishall station.

Coltishall/Horstead Pub Walk

On leaving the station walk down the B1150 Station Road in a southerly direction towards the centre of the village and just a few hundred yards on your right is The Railway Tavern.

The Railway Tavern

The Railway Tavern is an old Georgian style flint faced building with a red roof and old sash windows. It appears as though it was once two houses but there have been many alterations. A lantern over the doorway inscribed "The Norwich Brewery Company" reminds us that this was once a Watneys pub. There is a small beer garden at the front and a bigger one at the back, which includes a children's play area. Beers sold here today are mainly local coming from Humpty Dumpty, Wolf and Adnams. There is an extensive food menu. If you have time, go out to the back of the garden and look round the old disused Victorian Lime kiln which is reputedly one of the best preserved of its type in Norfolk and is a listed building. For more information on this pub look up website www.railwaycoltishall.co.uk

After leaving The Railway Tavern turn left towards Coltishall village down into High Street. When you come to the junction at the bottom of High Street, turn right over the humpback River Bure bridge into the parish of Horstead and on your right is The Recruiting Sergeant.

The Recruiting Sergeant is an old large roadside pub with whitewash and flint walls. The porch to the main entrance has a Dutch gable. There is a large car park at the front and a most attractive enclosed garden and patio at the rear. It has a spacious interior with a large bar and a separate room for dining. Real ales including Adnams beers are sold here.

The Recruiting Sergeant

When you leave The Recruiting Sergeant retrace your steps over the river bridge back into Coltishall, turn right into Church Street and proceed to walk through the main part of the village past the parish church and then shortly on your left you will come to the third pub on this walk The Red Lion.

The Red Lion

The Red Lion is a large rambling old 17th century inn with mustard coloured walls and a Dutch gable. Inside there are lots of old beams and different drinking areas on split-levels including a sunken bar. One room is a dining area. Beers on sale here are from Adnams, Bass plus guest ales.

To reach the last two pubs on this route continue along the B1354 in the Wroxham direction when you will soon come to The Kings Head and The New Rising Sun, which are next door to one another and close to the River Bure. The Kings Head is on the main road while The New Rising Sun is adjacent to the riverbank next to the mooring area for the Broads holiday cruisers. There is a large car parking area, which serves both pubs.

The Kings Head

The Kings Head is an old 17th century pub facing the main Coltishall to Wroxham road. It is a fine old building with Dutch gables and a long sloping roof. On the street side there appears to be an original ornate Georgian doorway leading into a richly decorated interior. On the parking side there is a large chimneystack and pretty bay windows with small panes and a small beer garden. There is an extensive food menu with meals available both lunchtimes and evenings. Real ales available here include Adnams, Marstons Pedigree plus guest(s). Because of its close proximity to the River Bure it can get busy during the tourist season particularly at evening meal times. It is open all day on Saturdays and Sundays. En-suite accommodation is available. For more information look up the pub's website which is www.kingshead.norfolkbroads.com

Across the car park is the New Rising Sun.

The New Rising Sun is a much bigger pub than its neighbour. It dates back to the mid 19th century. Adjoining is a restaurant called "The Granary Restaurant". There are commanding views of the River Bure. Many holiday cruisers moor up here in the holiday season. There is a large beer garden by the riverside. Here is a perfect place for a relaxed drink! Real ales available here come from Woodforde's, Greene King and Deuchars. This pub also has all day opening on Saturdays and Sundays.

New Rising Sun

After re-boarding the train at Coltishall Station you journey through a cutting and as the line gently bears right you will see the Network Rail "Bittern Line" converging on your left hand side. Here, after a total journey of some nine miles, is the end of the line. Wroxham Station is the eastern terminus of The Bure Valley Railway.

Hoveton/Wroxham

Despite being the unofficial capital of The Norfolk Broads and the most popular starting place for holiday makers making a cruise on the Broads, it is not very well endowed with pubs.

Wroxham Station

On exiting the station, turn left and take the footpath over the road and round the rear of the main line station. Go down a flight of steps and through the tunnel under the railway before turning right into Station Road, which will take you to the centre of town. Alternatively, instead of walking down Station Road you can turn in Roy's shopping car park and cross over to reach some pleasant gardens that border the river. This will bring you to the rear of The Kings Head Hotel by the riverbank.

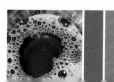

The
Kings Head

The Kings Head Hotel is a large red brick and flint building with a large rambling interior. It has a very large beer garden where you can eat and drink in summer and enjoy the views of the River Bure and the well-known road bridge crossing from Hoveton to Wroxham. The hotel is open and sells food all through the day. Real ales are available.

You can leave the Kings Head hotel by either the front or rear. Either way, it is only a few steps to the main A1151 Norwich-Stalham road. This is a busy road and you can take your life into your hands and cross over or retreat down the road to Roy's Shopping Centre and cross at the pelican crossing.

The small area here has a number of food outlets including fish & chip shops, a kebab house, tea rooms, ice cream parlours, Thai, Indian & Chinese restaurants plus an amusement arcade.

Before visiting the second pub, walk up the road to the famous humpback Wroxham Bridge and enjoy the view looking down the river at the many Broads cruisers and launches and swans, geese and ducks.

From the bridge retrace your steps a short way and on your right turn into Waterside Terrace, a pleasant pedestrian area with shops and more food outlets. Near the end of the street turn right and Hotel Wroxham is immediately in front of you.

Hotel Wroxham

Hotel Wroxham is a large modern hotel with a plush interior and easy chairs and settees and a typical hotel bar that sells real ales including Adnams Bitter, Broadside and Courage Best. Bar Snacks, a carvery and full restaurant meals are available. The bar is open all day. Alternatively in good weather go outside to "The Waterside Terrace, Bar and Restaurant" where you can drink and eat while watching the holidaymakers pass in their pleasure boats. The hotel offers en-suite accommodation. See pub website www.hotelwroxham.co.uk

On exhausting the pleasures of Wroxham you may retrace your steps along Station Road and catch a train back to Norwich.

The Bure Valley

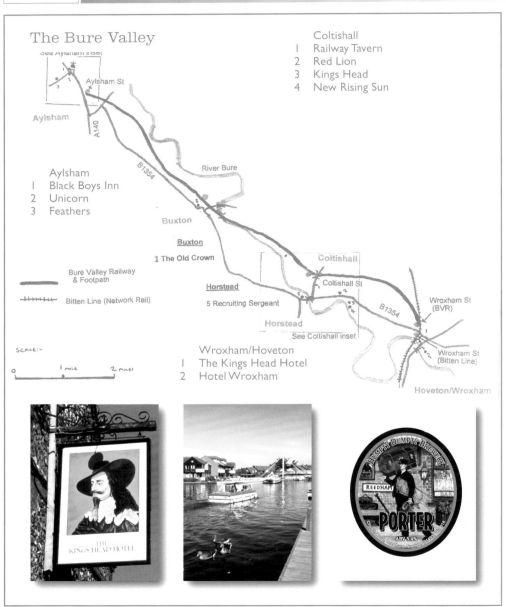

Coltishall
1. Railway Tavern
2. Red Lion
3. Kings Head
4. New Rising Sun

Aylsham
1. Black Boys Inn
2. Unicorn
3. Feathers

River Bure

Buxton

Buxton
1 The Old Crown

—— Bure Valley Railway
& Footpath

++++++ Bitten Line (Network Rail)

Horstead
5 Recruiting Sergeant

Horstead

SCALE:-

0   1 MILE   2 MILES

Coltishall

Coltishall St

See Coltishall inset

Wroxham St (BVR)

Wroxham St (Bitten Line)

Wroxham/Hoveton
1. The Kings Head Hotel
2. Hotel Wroxham

Hoveton/Wroxham

Wymondham Walk

Wymondham is an ancient market town situated some eight miles south west of Norwich and dates back to Anglo-Saxon times. The original Anglo-Saxon settlement was situated in the area around where a Saxon church once stood and where later the medieval Abbey was built. Wymondham was recorded in the Domesday Book (1087) as "Wimundham" and for those days was quite populous with nearly 700 inhabitants. Shortly after, Benedictine monks established a priory which grew to considerable size and wealth before its dissolution by Henry VIII.

Wymondham thrived in medieval times. The main industry was the woollen trade that brought prosperity to the area and remained important until the mid 19th century when it collapsed leaving great poverty in the town. The town's other major industry was wood and brush making that began in a small way during the Middle Ages but became a prominent employer by the 17th century and continued as one of the town's most important industries up to the mid 20th century and only declined in the 1950s with the last factory closing as recently as 1985. A reminder of the spoon and brush industry can be seen by the depiction of two domestic wooden implements at the bottom of the town sign situated on the corner of Church Street next to Becket's Chapel.

Wymondham's most famous hero was Robert Kett who led a rebellion in 1549 in protest to the enclosure of traditional lands. (See Norwich Pub Walk No 2 "Ketts Height Walk" for more of his history).

Market Cross

In 1615 there was a great fire in the town reputed to have been started by gypsies. Widespread destruction occurred in two areas around Middleton Street at the bottom of the High Street and at the other around The Market Cross and Bridewell Street at the top of The High Street. In all over 300 properties were destroyed including The Market Cross that dated back to 1220. The present Market Cross, which now serves as the Tourist Information Centre, was built in 1618.

By the early years of the 20th century the population of Wymondham was about 5,000 but this increased rapidly after the 1970s to a present day number of 12,500.

Getting There

Wymondham is easily accessible by both road and rail being on the main A11 trunk road between Norwich and London and on the railway line linking Norwich to Cambridge and Peterborough, the Midlands and the north. Regular train services between Norwich and Cambridge stop at Wymondham. There are also regular bus services to and from Norwich that pass through Wymondham enroute to Attleborough and Dereham. There are a few local services that connect with surrounding villages. Car parks are situated just off Market Street and also at the Railway Station although the latter tends to fill up on weekdays in the daytime as many people from Wymondham and nearby villages park here before commuting to Norwich by train.

The Walk

Leave Wymondham railway station and walk down a short hill, cross the main road and on your right is The Railway and the first pub on your walk. You may wish to start here and 'wet your whistle' before walking to the furthermost pub which is about fifteen minutes walking distance away.

The Railway dates back to the mid 19th century. It was originally known as The Dun Cow and then renamed The Railway Hotel after the coming of the railway to Wymondham. After a period of closure and refurbishment it reopened in March 2005 as 'The 'Railway'. The interior, which is on split levels,

The Railway

includes photos, railway memorabilia and pictures. There are around four different real ales on offer including, Adnams, Humpty Dumpty and Elgoods. There is a full varied food menu serving lunchtimes and evenings which includes main courses, (including many vegetarian dishes), bar snacks and a desert menu. The pub has a beer garden with a children's play area and a large car park. The pub website is www.therailwaypub.com

After leaving The Railway you may choose which order to visit the other Wymondham Pubs. We have elected to start at the furthest pub from the station which is The Feathers and then return. However you can walk in reverse or take any other order as you wish.

The Feathers is approximately fifteen minutes walk from the railway station. After leaving the station, head towards the town centre along Station Road. Cross at the traffic lights into Fairland Street and you will shortly emerge at the top of the main shopping area by The Market Cross. Walk down the narrow one-way Market Street that is lined with shops. The general impression is a 'quaint ' mixture of timbered structures and later Georgian and Victorian with a few modern buildings mixed in. At the end of Market Street the main road bears right. Follow it past a war memorial and on to Town Green where The Feathers is situated on your left hand side.

Records of The Feathers existing as a pub date back to the 18th century although much of the present building dates to early 19th century. The pub was formerly a Steward & Patteson and then a Watney pub and was once known as The Three Feathers. It is now a free house serving a large range of real ales which includes Adnams Bitter, Greene King Abbot and Marston's Pedigree, plus a number of guests. from a wide variety of breweries. The interior of the pub has cosy alcoves and on the walls are mounted entertaining memorabilia, some old farm implements and early photographs. There is even an old ARP warden's bicycle in one bar! The pub has a function room upstairs where a folk club meets monthly.

The Feathers

After leaving The Feathers retrace your steps towards the town centre. On the way you will pass a building that once housed a grammar school that is commemorated on a plaque. At the end of Middleton Street on you will see on your left "The Becket's Chapel" that dates to 1174. After the dissolution it was used for a variety of purposes and is now the Town's Library. Turn right here past the town sign into Church Street. Immediately on your right is the Green Dragon.

The Green Dragon dates back to late 15th century although much of its exterior is Tudor and half-timbered with a dormer window. It was lucky to have survived only superficial damage in the great fire of 1615 and one can still see scorch marks on external timbers. The interior retains some of the old features such as beams and

The Green Dragon

mantelpiece. Today's pub has a bar and a little snug with wooden pew type furniture and a small dining area on one side. Real ales sold here include Adnams Bitter & Broadside plus Greene King Old Speckled Hen plus guests which often include Wolf beers. It has a bar and full restaurant menu. Bed & Breakfast is available.

After enjoying a drink at The Green Dragon and before proceeding to the Market Place it is well worth making a short detour to have a look at the town's most famous building, Wymondham Abbey.

On leaving The Green Dragon turn right along Church Street. The road then bends sharp right and the large impressive Abbey will come into view. Founded in 1107 by William d'Albini, it was built to serve both as a monastery and a church for the people of Wymondham. However relations between monks and townsfolk got so bad that a six feet thick wall was built across the church dividing it into two. At the dissolution in 1538, the people of Wymondham purchased the Abbey. Today only the main Abbey survives with its two large impressive towers while ruins indicate the extent of the once flourishing monastery.

Wymondham Abbey

To return to the main walk after your visit to the Abbey, retrace your steps back to Church Street, past the Green Dragon and then turn right at the end of the road and back into Market Street. The next pub, The Heart of Wymondham, is immediately across the road on your right.

The Heart of Wymondham

The Heart of Wymondham was originally known as The White Hart and is of typical Georgian design. In the 18th and early 19th centuries it was Wymondham's main coaching inn. Note the large archway to the left of the pub leading to what were once the stables. During this period it was also a centre of entertainment where wrestling, music and other sports contests were promoted. Todays pub is a fairly trendy young persons pub with plenty of piped music, fruit machines etc. It does though have one quiet room that was once The Masonic Room and is now a dining area. The architecture in this room is very unusual having a classical theme with Grecian arches. Real ales on sale here include Adnams Bitter & Broadside plus Fullers London Pride.

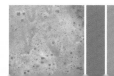

When leaving The Heart of Wymondham turn left and continue up Market Street and past The Market Cross an old octagonal shaped timber building with a pyramid roof that is supported by eight timber buttresses. It was built in 1617 after the great fire to replace a previous structure that dated to the 13th century. It is now the town's tourist information office.

Adjacent The Market Cross is the next pub of the walk The Cross Keys.

The Cross Keys

The Cross Keys dates back to the 16th century. The exterior is half-timbered with lead light windows and dormer windows set in the high-pitched roof. The original pub was on the left hand side and the right hand side where the main bar is today was only incorporated into the pub as recently as 1965. Inside there are old beams and wooden furniture. Real ales available here are from Adnams, Wolf Brewery and Fullers London Pride.

When you leave The Cross Keys, cross over the top of the Market Place go past the Market Cross, and turn right down Bridewell Street. The Queen's Head is a little way along the street on your right.

The Queen's Head is another old inn situated at the top of Bridewell Street near the top of the Market Place. The original timbers of the building date to just after the great fire of 1615, but most of the present exterior is Victorian with the exception of the main entrance that dates back to the 1600s. The pub was owned by the Diss Brewery from around 1800 but later became a Lacons and then a Whitbred house. It was used as the meeting place for 'The Agincourt Lodge of Manchester Independent Oddfellows' in the late 19th and early 20th century. A selection of real ales is available which include Adnams Bitter and Fullers London Pride.

The Queen's Head

After leaving The Queen's Head, turn right down Bridewell Street until you come to the end of the street where you will see a large Georgian building The Bridewell which was the town's prison and dates to 1785. There was a previous prison on this site dating to 1598. In time it was adapted to a police station, and later the town's Magistrates Court before becoming Wymondham's heritage museum in the mid 1990s.

When you reach The Bridewell, turn left and proceed along Norwich Road and about 300 yards on your left and setback from the main road is The Windmill, the last pub of the walk.

The Windmill is another very old pub thought to date back to the 16th century. The interior contains many old wooden beams. A small range of real ales are available.

The Windmill

To return back to the railway station, retrace your steps back past The Bridewell. Turn left and cross the main road at the traffic lights and walk back along Station Road until you come to the station on your right.

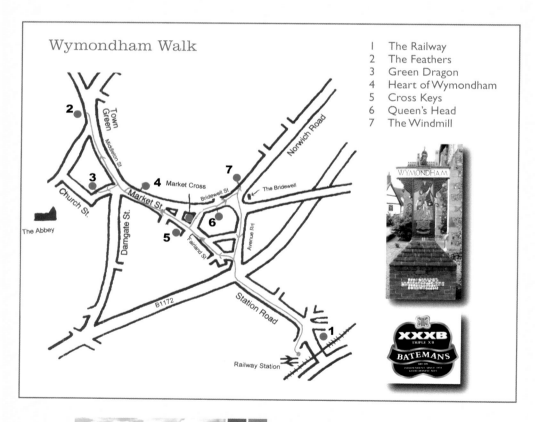

Wymondham Walk

1 The Railway
2 The Feathers
3 Green Dragon
4 Heart of Wymondham
5 Cross Keys
6 Queen's Head
7 The Windmill

Attleborough Walk

Attleborough is a small market town situated in south Norfolk, 15 miles south west of Norwich and 14 miles north east of Thetford.

Attleborough was settled, probably in the 5th century by Germanic invaders and became a part of the kingdom of East Anglia. The Domesday Book (1086) records its name as Atleburc, translated as the stronghold of the family called Aelta (i.e. name + beorg).

Attleborough survived troublesome times of tribal warfare, Viking invasions and Norman occupation to thrive in medieval times when Norfolk was one the most densely populated regions of England and the woollen industry its most important asset. A great fire in 1559 which started in the stables of The Griffin Hotel destroyed most of the town.

Attleborough
Town
Sign

In the 18th century stagecoaches & Royal Mail coaches changed horses on the turnpike road running between Norwich to London. This activity declined after 1845 with the building of a railway connection between Norwich to Brandon thus linking the town with train services from Norwich to London via Cambridge.

The market established in 1226, became famous in the 19th century as a centre for the sale of turkeys, (some while before Bernard Matthews came onto the scene!). This lasted well into the 20th century for in 1935 it is recorded that 7,000 birds were sold at Michaelmass.

In the 1850s Attleborough was a small town relying mainly on agriculture for its economy and had a population of 2,300 which only rose to just over 3,000 by the mid 1960s. The last three decades however has seen rapid development with its present population rising to over 7,500. It is now largely a 'dormitory' town being well situated close to Norwich and there are good road and rail connections with Cambridge. A new industrial estate, providing some local employment has grown up on the southeast side of town where the famous Gaymers cider factory stood between 1896 until it shut in 1995. The Wolf Brewery, established in 1996, one of Norfolk's best known independent breweries, is situated along with many other commercial outlets on part of the old Gaymers site.

Getting There

Attleborough, by Norfolk standards, is well served by road and rail. There are two railway services that pass through Attleborough. East Midlands Trains service from Norwich to Ely, Peterborough the Midlands and the North passes through Attleborough, as does National Express service between Norwich and Cambridge. Bus services between Norwich and Watton (X3) and Norwich to Bury St Edmunds (X4) pass through Attleborough town centre

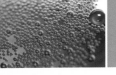

and there are a number of local services linking the town with nearby villages. Being just off the A11 trunk road between Norwich and London, Attleborough is easy to get to by road and there are plenty of car parks around the town.

The Walk

The walk starts at the Railway Station on Station Road. If arriving by train from the Norwich direction, when leaving the platform turn left and proceed over the level crossing and follow the road towards the town centre. If arriving from the Thetford or parking in the station car park turn right into station Road and proceed towards the town centre.

Walk on the right hand side along the wide Station Road. This was once the posh district with grand Victorian and Edwardian detached houses and landscaped gardens of trees and shrubs. You will come to the one-way road traffic system and on the corner is The Mulberry Tree, the first pub of the walk.

This building that was built in the late 19th century has an exterior design that is astonishingly ornate, typical of buildings built in this period. This pub was originally known as The New Inn but later renamed The Royal Hotel in 1888, a name which it retained until the 1990s when it became The Mulberry Tree. Today the ground floor interior has a large restaurant with a bar to one side. Real ales sold here are from the local Wolf Brewery and other guests.

The Mulberry Tree

Opposite The Mulberry Tree is a small traffic island with an obelisk bearing the word "Peace," dated 1856 with the names of four battles of the Crimean War; Alma, Sebastopol, Balaclava and Inkerman. The plinth at the base of the monument lists the mileages of 24 nearby towns and villages. If not unique this monument is most odd. Cross the road to the left and walk along Connaught Road passing more Victorian buildings and a large lovely thatched cottage. The road joins the ancient main street at High Street.

Bear left along the High Street and cross at the pedestrian lights. Pass the unsightly Sainsburys Garage and you will arrive at the second pub of the route, The Cock Inn.

The Cock Inn

The Cock Inn is an old building that dates back to at least to the 18th century, possibly earlier. In the 18th and early 19th centuries it was a staging post being conveniently situated on the old London road (the route of the Norwich to London turnpike), with stabling facilities for 70 horses. It has old sash windows and a Georgian doorway. It was previously a Bullards, Steward & Patteson's and then a Watneys pub. We are reminded that it was once a Watneys pub by a lantern at the doorway advertising "The Norwich Brewing Company". Today it is a cosy town pub consisting of two bars. Beers on sale here include Adnams and Woodforde's.

On leaving The Cock Inn, retrace your steps into the town centre along Exchange Street with its narrow pavements. Exchange Street has a low profile with long terraced rows of two storey buildings that are now mainly shops that originated as far back as the 17th century. On the right side and as part of a long terrace is The Bear, the next pub on the route.

The Bear is an old building whose first recorded license goes back to 1789. More recently it has undergone some refurbishment. The interior consists of one main bar with stone floors, exposed beams and an inglenook fireplace, plus a small snug with carpets and comfortable armchairs at the rear of the pub. There is a fair choice of real ales available supplied by a range of different brewers.

The Bear

After departing The Bear, continue along Exchange Street then after which you will enter Church Street. Note a large Victorian edifice that was originally the town Corn Exchange and reading room. At this point the character of the town alters and becomes a wide square with an attractive Green. At the far end of the Green is the Town Hall, an attractive Georgian house but as seems normal in Attleborough just another terrace. The Green has an attractive signboard, (complete with turkeys). There is also a war memorial. The plinth lists some 101 names of men who were killed in the First World War along with 24 names from the Second World War. The 101 casualties of the 1st World War is a significant number considering that the population at that time was only just over 2,000!

Opposite the Green is The London Tavern, the next pub of the route.

The London Tavern is a pub with a modern façade of what must be an older building. The interior consists of a large long one-room bar with stone floors and a pool table at one end. There is also a function room upstairs that is used as a disco at weekends. Real ales sold here come from the local Wolf Brewery.

The London Tavern

Just a short distance further along Church Street is The Griffin Hotel, the last pub on your route.

The Griffin Hotel was a former coaching inn with parts of the building dating back to the 16th century although substantial extensions were made during the 17th century. Like The Cock this was an important staging post on the London to Norwich turnpike (established 1695) where horses were changed and passengers took refreshments. The present pub consists of a main bar plus a smaller bar and dining area at the rear. Real ales include beers from Greene King plus many guests. Local beers being most prominent and there are always Wolf Beers available.

The Griffin Hotel

The Griffin Hotel is our last call and is next to St Mary's Church, largely Norman, and built c1100 on the foundations of an earlier Saxon church. This is an absolute gem. The 15th century screen has been described as "one of the most precious possessions of our English Churches", with a richly covered rood loft and 24 painted shields depicting the English Bishoprics of the day. There are also painted figures and wall paintings. Breathtaking, and worth a visit before returning home!

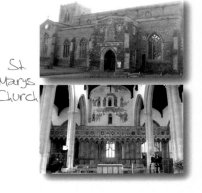

St. Marys Church

To return to your starting point, turn right down Surrogate Street, passing the Crimean War Memorial and down Station Road.

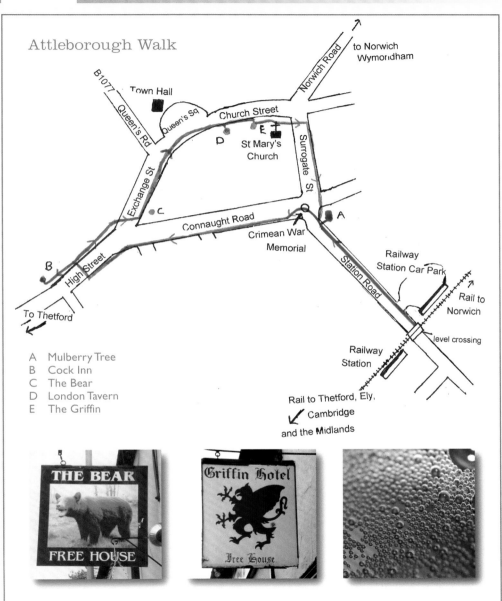

Attleborough Walk

to Norwich
Wymondham

Norwich Road

B1077

Queen's Rd

Town Hall

Queen's Sq

Church Street

St Mary's
Church

E

D

Surrogate St

Exchange St

C

Connaught Road

Crimean War
Memorial

A

Railway
Station Car Park

Station Road

Rail to
Norwich

High Street

B

level crossing

To Thetford

Railway
Station

Rail to Thetford, Ely,
Cambridge
and the Midlands

A   Mulberry Tree
B   Cock Inn
C   The Bear
D   London Tavern
E   The Griffin

Diss Pub Walk

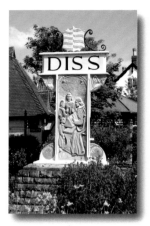

Diss Sign

Diss is a market town, situated on the Norfolk Suffolk border about mid distance between Norwich, Ipswich and Bury St Edmunds. The original settlement, which dates back to medieval times surrounds 'The Mere', a small lake, about 10,000 years old which dates back to the end of the last ice age. Although the town has grown over the centuries it is around this area that our pub walk takes place, finishing at Fair Green, just to the south west of the town centre.

Getting There

The most convenient way of travelling to Diss by public transport is by train. Diss is well positioned being on the main Norwich to London (Liverpool St) mainline, although there is nearly a mile walk from the railway station to the town centre. If you are travelling to Diss by bus, the bus station is on Park Road (marked 'B') on map close to the start of the walk. Alternatively if you are coming by car the most convenient car park to use is the one on Park Road (A1066, marked CP on map).

The Walk

The walk starts at the bottom of Mere Street at the junction with Park Road and Victoria Road. Walk up Mere Street in the direction of St Mary's Church. Before you arrive at the first pub pause just before the tourist information office where there is a viewpoint of The Mere where you can admire the view and see the numerous ducks and geese that frequent this area. Continue a few yards up the street and on the left you come to The Waterfront, the first pub of the route.

Diss Mere

This 17th century pub was formerly known as The Sun Inn until 2003 when it assumed its present name. The interior consists of a number of interconnecting rooms, many of which have undergone much recent refurbishment. The front room has a low beamed ceiling. Further on you will walk through into the main bar and through to a conservatory which opens out to a beer terrace with commanding views of The Mere. Beers on sale here come from the Greene King Brewery and include IPA, Abbot and Old Speckled Hen.

The Waterfront

On leaving The Waterfront turn left and walk up the hill towards the Market Place until just before the Church and on your left is The White Horse, the second pub on the route. Notice before you enter the pub on the opposite side is of a fine old timber framed building, 'The Dolphin House', which dates back to the 16th century and was once the house of a wealthy merchant.

The White Horse

Situated at the top end of The Market Place, this old pub dates back to at least the early 19th century and probably before. This small one bar pub is L-shaped and has a friendly atmosphere. There is an upstairs function room. Real ales on offer here are supplied by Adnams, with. Bitter and Broadside usually available.

Leave the White Horse, cross the street, turn left and The Saracens Head will emerge into view on your right hand side.

This grade II listed building was originally the hall of The Weavers Guild and is a legacy that reminds us of the prosperous past of Diss when in medieval times it was an important commercial woollen centre. Beers sold here are usually from East Anglian brewers such as Adnams and Greene King. The pub has a very varied menu which includes both bar food and an a la carte menu. For more details see www.saracensheaddiss.co.uk. The pub also has accommodation with single, double and family rooms available.

The Saracens Head

The Greyhound

Leave The Saracens Head and retrace your steps back to the junction with St Nicholas Street and proceed a few yards along the street until you come to on the right hand side, the next pub on the route, The Greyhound. Situated at the top end of Diss Mere this building dates back to the 17th century although there was a pub on this site in the 15th century. It was an ex Bullards and then Watney house. It has a comfortable bar with widescreen TV for live sports. There is a separate dining room. Real ales sold here come from by Wolf Brewery.

After leaving The Greyhound, your next pub is only a few yards further along St Nicholas Street, The Two Brewers.

The Two Brewers

This old inn dates from the 18th century and has a white exterior with black beams. It was once owned by the long defunct Diss Brewery before being taken over by Lacons and then Adnams. It is now been taken over by Scottish & Newcastle. There is a wide screen TV for showing live sports.

Turn right from The Two Brewers, and walk to the end of St Nicholas Street where on the junction with Denmark Street, straight in front of you is the next pub of the walk, The Crown,

It is a large red bricked building with some mock Tudor beams on the external walls. The present building dates from the 1870s but there was a pub on this site previously. At one time it was a Watneys pub that was taken over by Brent Walker in late 1980s and is now owned by Punch Taverns. The interior consists of one large bar with a pool table. A small range of real ales are available.

The Crown

From the Crown, turn right and walk down Denmark Street. You will catch glimpses of The Mere in between the houses on your left as you walk down the street until near the bottom on the right hand side you arrive at The Park Hotel.

The Park Hotel

This is a large Georgian building with an impressive semi circular porch at the entrance. Although essentially a hotel with seventeen rooms there is a bar open to non residents that sells Adnams Bitter. For more information consult their website www.parkhotel-diss.co.uk

When departing The Park Hotel turn right and continue to the bottom of Denmark Street. Cross Park Road at the mini roundabout and then proceed to the junction with Lower Denmark Street. Walk along Lower Denmark Street. With a terrace of old houses on your left and an old maltings on your right you will eventually emerge onto Fair Green, a rural suburb on the south west side of Diss which consists of a large green surrounded by many old houses. About half way down the Green on the left hand side is The Cock Inn, the last pub on the route.

This charming old 16th century building that overlooks Fair Green has many old beams, a tiled floor and a real log fire. The rambling interior consists of many seating areas that have an eclectic mix of unmatched large armchairs. There is wide screen TV for live sports. Old photos of the pub seem to suggest that it once had a thatched roof. Beers sold here are Adnams Bitter, Fullers London Pride, Taylors Landlord plus guests. Food is served Monday to Friday lunchtimes and Thursday to Saturday evenings.

The Cock Inn

To return back to the start, retrace your steps to Park Road and continue along past the car park on your left and bus station on your right, and you will soon arrive back at the bottom of Mere Street, and you will be at the start having completed a full circuit of Diss Mere.

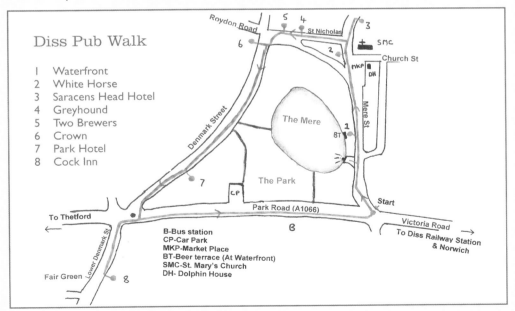

Diss Pub Walk

1 Waterfront
2 White Horse
3 Saracens Head Hotel
4 Greyhound
5 Two Brewers
6 Crown
7 Park Hotel
8 Cock Inn

B-Bus station
CP-Car Park
MKP-Market Place
BT-Beer terrace (At Waterfront)
SMC-St. Mary's Church
DH- Dolphin House

Fakenham Pub Walk

The market town of Fakenham is situated in the upper Wensum valley in North West Norfolk about 25 miles north west of Norwich, 22miles north east of Kings Lynn and about 12 miles south of Wells. The town is Saxon in origin dating from the 6th century and according to a book of Place Names its name derives from the homestead of a man called Facca. The Domesday Book (1086) records the name of Fakenham having "three mills, half a salt house, a flour mill and 200 sheep". From other data the population can be estimated at around 100. Fakenham evidently prospered for in the mid 13th century it was granted a charter to hold a weekly market on Thursdays.

By 1801 the town's population had grown to 1,236 and continued to grow during the Victorian era. Local economy was boosted by Thomas Miller who started a printing business that expanded and lasted well into the 20th century and is survived today by a few printing firms.

An even greater boost was the arrival in 1849 of a branch railway line from Wymondham that linked Fakenham to the main Norwich-Cambridge line. Then in the 1880s Fakenham acquired another line running east west from Kings Lynn to Melton Constable that was eventually extended to the east coast at Yarmouth and was later known as the M & GN (Midland & Great Northern) line.

Today the town of Fakenham is a lovely small market town with a population of about 6,500 that was recently voted by "Country Life Magazine" as the seventh best place in the country to live in. Several narrow streets lined with small shops and outlets for agencies lead to the hub of Fakenham that is the market square. Every Thursday on market day it comes to life when the square is covered with brightly coloured stalls and the car parks are full and hundreds of shoppers descend on the town.

Thursday is market day

Getting There

The railway connections to Fakenham are long gone when both lines were closed in the late 1950s-early 60s. However, there are many bus services. Service X56 connects Fakenham with Norwich. X98 Service which runs between Kings Lynn and the north Norfolk coast to Sheringham and Cromer passes through Fakenham. Connections to Wells and Walsingham are provided via Service 431. There are also a number of rural bus services serving surrounding villages.

If travelling by car there are several car parks close to the town centre, the best ones being either near Highfield Road on the northern approach to the town or the one just off Bridge Street in the town centre.

The Walk

We begin our walk at the north end of the town and proceed towards the Market Place in the somewhat narrow Oak Street. You will soon reach the first pub on your left, The Star.

The Star

Set back from the main road this hidden gem can easily be missed. The Star is the oldest surviving pub in Fakenham. Note the 17th century gables and two storey porch at the front of this flint and brick building. Once inside this old locals inn with its original beams and fine panelling you will receive a warm and friendly welcome. There is a pool table and other pub games. A rotating range of two real ales are usually available. The pub does not provide food. There is a large child friendly beer garden at the rear of the pub.

On leaving The Star, turn left and continue along Oak Street towards the Market Place. There are a number of bus stops on the left and a new Tesco superstore on the right. Our second call is The Oak Inn to your right on the corner just before the street bears left into the Market Place.

The Oak Inn is a restaurant pub. This fine building, which was once known as Cawdron House, has recently undergone extensive refurbishment. It is very spacious inside and there is a beer terrace at the rear. There is an extensive restaurant menu. Real ales sold here include Adnams Bitter and Greene King Old Speckled Hen. Note there is a sign on the front door informing customers of dress code "smart, casual only".

The Oak Inn

When leaving The Oak Inn, cross the street towards The Hollywood Cinema and continue into The Market Place where the street widens. The Market Place is an open space with three island buildings in the centre. The first is The Hollywood Cinema that you will see as you leave The Oak Inn. This Victorian building was originally the important Corn Exchange where farmers sold corn to merchants. Alas it became a Bingo hall before being converted into a cinema. Beyond, the Market Place is split by the other two island buildings which are banks. The open areas are filled with stalls on market day.

Nearly opposite and to the left of the Hollywood Cinema up a small lane is the magnificent medieval parish church of St Peter and St Paul with its lofty tower with belfry and clocks that chime the quarter hour. The buildings around the square are a mixture of Georgian and Victorian architecture. One large building is the Aldiss Department Store established in 1892 as a drapery shop that expanded and is now one of the few independent department stores left in the country. Of interest are the original engravings on the façade with catch phrases such as "Large stock always kept" and "Best Value always given".

It is worth while to amble around the Square and gaze in shop windows and take in the fine architecture which was the result of rebuilding after the medieval town was ravished by no less than three fires in the late 17th and early 18th century. At the far end of the Square, on the right you will come to The Crown Hotel, a fine example of an 18th century coaching Inn.

This old coaching inn dates back to the 18th century. It has been known as The Crown since 1795. There are a large number of eating and drinking areas including a conservatory called "The Sun Terrace". Real ales including Adnams Bitter are available. There is a restaurant and bar menu available using locally sourced produce wherever possible. High quality ensuite rooms are available. The hotel has its own car park. For more information see hotel website www.crownhotelfakenham.co.uk

The Crown Hotel

As you come out of the Square you will see on your right 'Benbows', a fruit and veg shop with its dominating Dutch gable and an enormous Georgian gable window. Turn right into the narrow Bridge Street with its small shops and on your left is Miller Walk a shopping arcade. After a short walk along the street you will arrive at The Bull on your left.

The Bull

This pub was completely refurbished in 2004. The interior is open plan with many tables, chairs and comfortable sofas. A range of around five real ales is available- Woodforde's Wherry and Elgood's Black Dog Mild plus a rotating range of three guests that are often from local micros such as Buffy's, Tipples and Fox. There is a lunchtime menu including a family area where children are welcome. Accommodation is available with ensuite rooms. For more information see www.thefakenhambull.co.uk

On leaving The Bull it is only necessary to cross the road to The Garden House.

The Garden House

Formally known as "The Limes" this establishment has recently reverted to its former name after recent extensive refurbishment. It is very much "the young persons" venue with karaoke on Mondays and live music with DJs on weekend evenings when it apparently gets very lively. There is a games room extension with pool table, large TV screen and electric games machines. Real Ales available include Adnams Broadside.

After leaving The Garden House, turn right and continue down Bridge Street. Bear right at the mini roundabout past some new residential homes and it is only a short walk to The Wensum Lodge Hotel which is to the right just before the bridge over The River Wensum.

This building is a pure gem, sited opposite a large mill pond shaded by willows. It was originally a grain store situated next to the old water mill. Now it is a converted hotel and restaurant with large bars and dining areas. There are lovely views of the old water mill and River Wensum from the dining area at the back. There is a large beer garden at the rear of the hotel, and a small car park at the front. Real ales available here are Greene King IPA and Abbot. See www.wensumlodge.co.uk

The Wensum Lodge Hotel

On leaving The Wensum Lodge take a look at the flowing mill pond and the mill race that emerges from under the large mill now converted into flats and evidently "saved for future generations" by the foresight of Derek Easter. At the far side of the mill is a weir holding back a substantial body of the Wensum River. The Wensum Lodge Hotel is the last pub on this walk but if you wish to try another there is The Rampant Horse on Queens Road. Retrace your steps back to The Market Place and turn right into Norwich Street.

The Rampant Horse is an unpretentious back street local mainly for the younger clientele with large TV screen for live sports. It is uncertain whether real ale is available.

Alternatively cross The River Wensum and take a trip back in time and visit The Gas Works Museum, which dating back to 1846 is the only surviving gas works in England and Wales. It is complete with all the equipment used to manufacture gas from coal. There is also a local history museum on the same site.

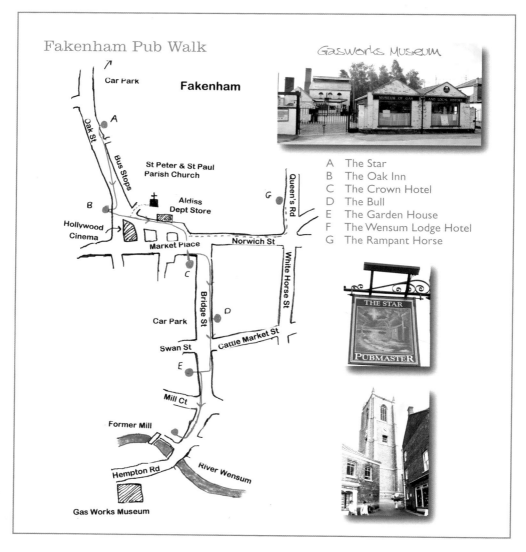

Fakenham Pub Walk

Gasworks Museum

Fakenham

A   The Star
B   The Oak Inn
C   The Crown Hotel
D   The Bull
E   The Garden House
F   The Wensum Lodge Hotel
G   The Rampant Horse

THE STAR
PUBMASTER

Dereham Pub Walk

Dereham or East Dereham as it was previously known is a busy market town situated in the centre of Norfolk about 20 miles west of Norwich and 25 miles east of King's Lynn.

The town's origins go back to the 7th century when King Anna, an Angle king, was killed at the battle of Blythburgh in A.D. 654 and his daughter, Withburga fled and founded a nunnery on what was later to become the site of present day Dereham. In 974 after her remains were stolen by the Abbot of Ely, there was a legend that a spring opened up at the site of the empty tomb whose waters were said to

Dereham Town Sign

have healing properties. Today there is a well known as "St Withburga's Well" in the churchyard of the Norman 12th century St Nicholas Parish Church. As it was sacked and destroyed by Danes in 870 the exact site of the nunnery is unknown.

Dereham had evidently flourished for it is recorded in The Domesday Book that the estimated population was about 250 with 3 Water Mills and 20 pigs. A medieval market was established in the 13th century and by the 16th century the population had risen to around 1,000. Leather, cloth and agricultural produce dominated the economy at this period.

One of Dereham's most infamous residents was Edmund Bonner born 1500, and ordained a priest by Cardinal Wolsey. He became Rector of Dereham 1534-1538 and after the accession of Mary Tudor in 1553 he became Bishop of London. During her reign over 270 protestant 'heretics' were burnt at the stake and it is said that Bishop Bonner was responsible for at least 200 of them. In 1558, when Elizabeth I came to the throne, he was relieved of his duty and thrown into prison where he died in 1569. The thatched cottage he lived in while Rector of Dereham is next to the Parish Church, and now a museum.

Dereham suffered two great fires, one in 1581 which destroyed nearly 400 homes and another in 1659 destroying about 170 homes which, with the exception of the Parish Church and Bonner's cottage, means that the buildings around the market are no older than late 17th century. The 19th century saw a large rise in the town's population. In 1811 the population had risen to 2,200 partly as a result of the building of the Swaffham to Norwich turnpike at the end of the 18th century. After the coming of the railways in the 1840s Dereham grew even more prosperous and the population reached 5,500 by the end of the century.

Today, Dereham has a population of 13,300 and it is one of Norfolk's major market towns with many large retail businesses and it is also the administrative centre for the Breckland District Council.

The Walk

The walk begins on the east side of the High Street where the bus stops are located. Dereham High Street consists of mainly Georgian buildings hidden at ground level by shop fronts that have been unsympathetically modernised and bare little resemblance of the original street. From the bus stops cross over High Street and walk through the narrow Red Lion Road towards Quebec Street at the other end of this short street you will find the first pub of the route, The Red Lion on your right.

The Red Lion is a small cosy friendly back street town centre local. Records of this pub date back to as early as 1727. The interior comprises of one long bar that has a dart board at one end. There are a number of widescreen TVs for live sports. The walls are covered with old photos of Dereham. There are usually two real ales available including Hobgoblin and a guest. Opening hours are Mon-Sat 10-11.30, Sun 12-10.30. No food is available but there are plenty of restaurants, cafes and fast food outlets in and around The Market Place.

The Red Lion

When leaving The Red Lion, turn left into Quebec Street and then right into Church Street. You will see St Nicholas Parish Church in front of you at the end of Church Street. The Phoenix Hotel, pub number two is on your right hand side about half way down the street.

The Phoenix Hotel

Situated very close to the parish church this large hotel was built in 1963. It has a number of split level drinking areas including a library area complete with leather bound books. Real ales on offer here include Greene King IPA, Old Speckled Hen and Ruddles County. Being a hotel it offers a full hotel food menu lunchtimes and evenings as well as a bar menu and is open from 11-11 each day. As this public house has recently been purchased by Wetherspoons so range of beers available may alter.

St. Nicholas Church

After visiting The Phoenix and before preceding to the next pub it is well worth continuing to the end of the street to St Nicholas Parish Church which dates from Norman times although there were additions in the later medieval period and others more recent. St Withburga's Well is situated in the western end of the churchyard behind the church.

Just round the corner from the church in St Withburga's Lane is "Bonner's Cottage".

"Bonner's Cottage"

This fine old timber frame and reed thatched cottage with its low doorways has some unusual decoration under the eaves known as pargetting. It was built in the early 16th century, was once the residence of Bishop Bonner, (as mentioned in the introduction). Today it is a local museum.

After visiting The Parish Church and Bonner's Cottage, return back to the High Street via Church Street into the Market Place passing a cinema which was originally The Corn Hall built in 1856 after the coming of the railways which brought new wealth to the town. It closed as a corn exchange in 1927. When you reach High Street turn right. A short distance on your left past many shops is The Bull, the next pub of the walk.

The Bull is a Greene King pub dating back to the 17th century and was once a Steward & Patteson pub closed by Watneys in 1969. The present pub opened in 1974. The interior consists of a number of interconnecting rooms including a games room with TV screens and pool table. It has a fine garden patio at the rear of the building which is a great place to go in the summer months. Beers include Greene King IPA and Abbot Opening hours are Mon-Thurs 11-11, Fri-Sat 11-12 and Sun 12-11. Food available each lunchtimes 12-3 and there are themed food evenings including curry nights on Mondays.

The Bull

After leaving The Bull, turn left and continue down the High Street where you will pass many more shops and other retail premises. At the small roundabout continue straight on into Baxter Row. You will shortly come to The Royal Standard, which is on the right hand side of the street.

The Royal Standard

The building which dates from the 17th century was originally known as The Light Horse but under this name it was closed by Watneys in 1975. It reopened as a free house in 1982 assuming its present name from another closed pub in -The Royal Standard. There is one main bar with low exposed beams; open fires red tiled floors with lots of wooden chairs and tables. There is a second bar that acts as a games room with pool table and widescreen TV which looks onto a beer large garden. Although not a Greene King pub the beers are supplied by Greene King and include IPA, Abbot and Speckled Hen. Opening hours are Mon-Thurs 10-midnight, Fri-Sat 10 1am, Sun 12-10.30.

When leaving The Royal Standard, return back along Baxter Row and into the High Street once again. Turn right, then proceed along Norwich Street. Cross straight over the junction with Cowper Road at the traffic lights and The Kings Head is on your left.

The Kings Head Hotel, built in the early 18th century, has one large lounge bar plus a small function room. Meals are served in the adjoining dining room. The bar opens out onto a large garden which is set out with tables and chairs during the summer months. The bar is run by an enthusiastic Tunisian who is very knowledgeable and proud of his real ales. Greene King IPA and Abbot, Adnams Broadside plus rotating guest beers are available. The hotel hosts occasional beer festivals. Opening hours are Mon-Sat 11-11 and Sun 12-10.30.

The Kings Head

After leaving The King's Head you have a choice. First you may continue along Norwich Street and then over the next traffic lights into Norwich Road where you can take in two additional pubs, The Coachmakers and The Crown.

If you are interested in heritage railways it is worth a walk to Dereham Railway Station, the Headquarters of The Mid Norfolk Railway. The Mid Norfolk Railway was opened in 1999 between Dereham and Wymondham, a distance of 11 miles, although at some time in the future it is hoped to run trains as far as North Elmham and County School to the north which will make the line over 17 miles in length. It runs services

Dereham Station

during the summer months on Wednesdays and Weekends operating mainly diesels and diesel multiple units with steam engines making the occasional guest appearances for short periods.

Alternatively, if you are not interested in additional pubs or The Mid Norfolk Railway, turn right on leaving The King's Head and return to High Street. Turn right at High Street, proceed through The Market to the roundabout at the north end of The Market and on your left at the beginning of Swaffham Road is the last pub of the walk, The George Hotel.

The George Hotel has a comfortable main bar which features wood panelling and pictures of local historical interest. There is also a conservatory and a patio to which you can take your drinks or food. The beer menu strongly emphasises local ales which include, Adnams Bitter and Broadside, Beeston Worth the Wait and on the Huh, Woodforde's Wherry plus guest ales. There is a full a la Carte restaurant an extensive bar menu available. The hotel has 8 ensuite rooms. Opening hours are Mon-Thurs, 10-11 Fri-Sat 10-midnight and Sun 10-11.

The George Hotel

Dereham Market Place

On leaving The George Hotel, if travelling by bus, return into The Market and the bus stops are on your right hand side.

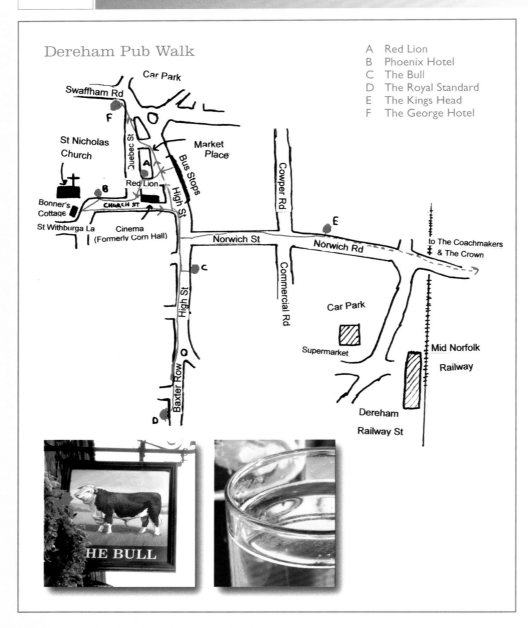

Dereham Pub Walk

A   Red Lion
B   Phoenix Hotel
C   The Bull
D   The Royal Standard
E   The Kings Head
F   The George Hotel

Car Park

Swaffham Rd

F

St Nicholas
Church

Quebec St

Market
Place

A

Bus Stops

Red Lion

B

Bonner's
Cottage

CHURCH ST

St Withburga La

Cinema
(Formerly Corn Hall)

High St

Cowper Rd

E

Norwich St

Norwich Rd

to The Coachmakers
& The Crown

C

High St

Commercial Rd

Car Park

Supermarket

Mid Norfolk

Railway

Baxter Row

D

Dereham
Railway St

Dereham

Great Yarmouth Pub Walk

At the time of the Roman occupation in the first century AD, the coastline was very different. The Rivers Bure, Yare and Waveney joined before flowing into the North Sea in a wide stretch of water called "The Great Estuary". Later when the region was harassed by Saxon pirates the Romans built Burgh Castle and Caister on opposite shores. Meanwhile, on a sandbank in the middle of the estuary, there were a few huts that were the beginning of Great Yarmouth.

In time, the sand bank expanded and merged with the Caister shore. Seven hundred years later Gt Yarmouth remained a small village when the Domesday Book (1087) recorded a population of only 70. Since then Gt Yarmouth developed sufficiently so that in 1209 King John granted a Charter. The wealth of the now flourishing town was founded in its trading port and herring fishing.

The position of Gt Yarmouth made it vulnerable to attack by land and sea and so in 1284 a start began on building a town wall. It was a substantial undertaking and took about 100 years to complete. The wall started at Southgate and went round in

Remains of Wall

wide arc to Northgate close to the confluence of The Bure and the Yare being 2,234 yards in length, 23 feet high and enclosing an area of 133 acres. It was further strengthened in 1625. The river was considered sufficient defence on the east side. When The English Civil War began in 1642, Gt Yarmouth declared for Parliament and the gates were kept locked but the war stayed a distance away. During the next century and after the wall fell into disrepair. Fortunately much of it has survived and today Gt Yarmouth has one of the most complete medieval walls of any town in England.

Regency Road

In the early 19th Century the Prince Regent began a trend which was to popularise seaside holidays. At first only the affluent visited Gt Yarmouth but the coming of railways brought families from industrial cities of the East Midlands and the North. Gt Yarmouth rose to the occasion and a whole new town grew up to the east by the sea. Furthermore the construction of Wellington Pier attracted more holiday makers on visiting Steam Packets. By the end of the 19th century Gt Yarmouth's economy was booming both from tourism and fishing. Then came the outbreak of World War I and a halt to holidays. Yarmouth was vulnerable again and in 1915 Gt Yarmouth was one of the first towns to suffer air raids.

After the war the holiday industry flourished again until 1939 at the start of World War II. Yarmouth was in the front line and was badly damaged from no less than 167 air raids between 1940-45, mostly by hit and run attacks across the North Sea from Holland.

$N^2B =$

Since 1945 the economy of Gt Yarmouth has taken a double blow. By the 1960s fishing had all but finished although its loss was partly offset by Gt Yarmouth becoming an offshore base for gas exploration in the North Sea. Tourism continued to play an important role in Yarmouth's economy until the 1970s when a decline set in because of the competition from cheap overseas package holidays. However, Gt Yarmouth has not entirely lost its popularity and during the summer season the front is thronged with visitors.

The Gardens on Great Yarmouth Seafront

Getting There

In the early and mid 20th century, the heyday of Yarmouth's tourist industry, the town was served by three railway stations. Now only Vauxhall Station survives offering regular services to and from Norwich. Bus service X1 from Peterborough to Lowestoft calls through Wisbech, Kings Lynn, Norwich and Yarmouth (at Market Gates) with a half hourly service during the day offering a good cross country connections. There are many local bus services connecting Yarmouth with Caister, The Broads, Cromer and the north Norfolk coast and with Gorleston and Lowestoft to the south.

The Walk

The walk starts at Gt Yarmouth Railway Station. This station was once known as Yarmouth Vauxhall in the days when Yarmouth had three terminus railway stations. A second was Yarmouth Beach, which was to the north of the town, (closed in 1959): part of The Midland & Great Northern Railway giving Yarmouth a direct link to the Midlands. The third was Yarmouth Southtown, (closed 1970) which linked Yarmouth with Lowestoft and also provided a direct rail service to London Liverpool St. which was particularly well used during the summer season.

Turn right when leaving the station and cross The River Bure via the steel girder bridge. Now a pedestrian bridge, it once carried a tramway that led to Yarmouth docks thereby giving the docks a direct rail link with the National Rail Network. With the demise of rail freight traffic it is now used as a footbridge. When you reach the end of the footpath turn left at "The Seafood Restaurant" (which is to your right), and proceed along North Quay towards the roundabout. Just before you reach the roundabout take a left turn along a footpath that leads towards the River Bure. Follow this footpath under the main road bridge. Tall people beware; there is only 5ft 9ins headroom under the bridge! When you emerge from under, The White Swan is in front to the right.

CAMRA
CAMPAIGN FOR REAL ALE

The White Swan

This pub was a former Steward & Patteson pub situated near the river and Yacht Centre and offers a range of about two real ales including Shepherd Neame Spitfire and John Smith's Bitter. It is open all day 11-11; 12-11 Sundays and food is available lunchtimes and evenings. The interior comprises two rooms, a lounge and a bar with a pool table. There is a pleasant outside drinking area at the front of the pub overlooking the river.

On the left of the pub is a Tower that once formed the North West gatehouse of the town's medieval walls. By the river bank is a footpath that leads to Gt Yarmouth Yacht Station, which is where Broad's holiday cruisers moor up when they stop at Yarmouth.

On leaving The White Swan retrace your steps for a short distance and then take the footpath that bears to the left. Follow signs "Town Centre" and proceed under "North Quay" underpass. After coming out of the underpass walk along Fuller's Hill to the next set of pelican crossings. Cross over and you will then enter the northern end of The Market Place. On your left you will have good views of Gt Yarmouth's Parish Church, St Nicholas, built in the early 12th century and the largest parish church in England with an area of 23,000 square feet. The Gallon Pot is in front of you on the right.

St. Nicholas

The Gallon Pot

An ex Lacons pub that was formerly known as "Burroughs Wine Lodge". The original building was destroyed during a bombing raid in 1943 and the present pub dates from the 1950s. It is ideally situated at the north end of the Market Place. The interior is open planned and spacious with a raised area at one end. There is a cellar bar where children with families are welcome. Because of its location on The Market Place this pub is often very busy at lunchtimes. Opening hours are: Mon-Sat, 10-midnight; & Sun 12-10.30. A large range of real ales are available including Adnams Bitter, Fullers London Pride, Greene King Old Speckled Hen and Woodforde's Wherry. Meals are available lunch and evenings.

121

After a refreshing drink leave The Gallon Pot and turn right and walk through the busy market place which is covered at the bottom (southern end). Continue through the covered area and past the numerous chip stalls. When you come to the end of the covered market turn left at "Help the Aged" shop into Market Gates and hidden just behind is The Feathers Hotel.

This pub is reputed to be the oldest pub in the town dating back to the 16th century. The pub has an original doorway through which Charles II allegedly walked. Once there was more than one bar but todays pub has been converted to make a single room although the old character remains. There is an open fire and internal exposed beams that gives a welcoming feel to the place. Real ales on offer include Adnams Bitter and John Smiths Bitter. Opening hours are Mon-Sat 10-11 & Sun 12-11.

The Feathers

On leaving The Feathers turn left and walk along Market Gates towards the traffic lights where you will see the redbrick "Market Gate" shopping complex on an upper level to your right. Also, before you reach the traffic lights you may note parts of the old town wall that are below "The Market Gates" shopping centre. Turn right at the traffic lights and proceed through the bus station and under the "Market Gates" shopping complex. The Troll Cart, the next pub on the route is on your left as you emerge from under Market Gates, which is on a corner of the pedestrianized Regent Road.

The Troll Cart

A J D Wetherspoon outlet called The Troll Cart was built as a new pub as part of The Market Gates complex in 1996. Its name derives from old hand carts that used to be pulled around the town. Opening hours are 9-12 midnight each day. Typical of the Wetherspoon's chain, the interior is one large open planned area with a number of different drinking areas. An ever changing range of about 8 real ales are usually available. Food is available from 9am-11pm providing the usual Wetherspoon fayre.

After leaving The Troll Cart bear left and walk down the pedestrian only Regency Road in the direction of the sea front. This street is full of cafes, clothes shops, gift shops, general bric-a-brac shops and CD shops blaring noisy Country & Western music. At the next major junction turn right and walk down Nelson Road Central. Here you will pass many small corner pubs too

122

numerous to list. You may wish to try some and if you are lucky you may find real ale. The street is mainly Victorian terraced housing with some commercial premises. Continue past St Georges recreation park and the children's playground. Cross over the mini roundabout at St Peter's Road, then turn right into the narrow and cobble stoned Malakoff Road. On the next corner you will arrive at The Red Herring on the right.

The Red Herring

This single friendly corner local has one bar that has a separate area with a pool table and wide TV screen for live sports. Opening hours are Mon-Fri 12-3 & 6-1am; Sat 11-1am & Sun 12-1am. The interior walls are adorned with many old photographs reminding us of Yarmouth's maritime history. Real ales available include the local Blackfriars Mild and Bitter, Fullers London Pride plus a changing range of guest ales some from local micros. No food is available but there is a fish & chip shop next door.

On leaving The Red Herring, turn right in the direction of "The Time & Tide Museum" which is just to your left. If you have spare time this award winning museum is well worth a visit. It is located in what once was a Victorian herring curing works and its attractive displays trace the history of Gt Yarmouth from the last Ice Age to the present day. It depicts Yarmouth's rich maritime traditions and the development of the herring industry up to modern times since Yarmouth became a popular seaside resort. For more information consult website www.museums.norfolk.gov.uk or tel 01493 743930.

Turn left at The Time and Tide Museum and proceed along Alma Road, and then take next right. In front and at the end of the street is St Spiridon Church, (a Victorian church originally known as St Peter's that in 1964 it became Greek Orthodox). Bear left at the church and cross over to Nottingham Way. Continue down Nottingham Way and after a short walk you will arrive at South Quay.

Turn right here and proceed along South Quay in a northerly direction towards The Haven Bridge. Here there are good views. On the far side of The River Yare are numerous wharfs and industrial premises. On your right is an interesting mix of Victorian buildings together with older and modern. Two buildings of particular note are The "Port & Haven Commissioners Office" with its intricate flint fronted building and an inscription on top dated 1909. The sides of the building are red bricked and are apparently much older dating back to the 16th century. A little further on and near The Haven Bridge is No 9 South Quay, a building with white façade, shared by a dentist's surgery and "The Quayside Plaza", a restaurant and bistro. Note the intricate design on the corner doorway dated 1890.

As you continue you will eventually reach Yarmouth Town Hall; an impressive red brick building built 1878-82 with its tall 110 foot tower.

Bear to the right and follow round the square to Nat West Bank where you will find a small alleyway that will take you directly to The Mariners Tavern.

This former Lacons pub has a charming old soft Norfolk red brick and flint exterior. Inside there are two rooms, a main bar and a wood panelled lounge with a pool table. There is a small outside drinking area. No food is available. Opening hours are Mon-Thurs 11-midnight, Fri-Sat 11-1AM & Sun 12-11. There is an ever changing range of about 8 ales many of which come from local micros. Note on the wall outside a notice board that not only advertises the current beers available but also those that a shortly to be available listed as "nearly born".

The Mariners Tavern

After leaving The Mariners turn left and walk along Howard Street South and then left into Stonecutters Way when you will arrive at the main road at North Quay. Turn right and walk along North Quay and you will very shortly arrive at St Johns Head the last pub of this walk and your final destination.

The St Johns Head is reputed to be built on land confiscated from monks of the Carmelite Order and ales have been served on this site for over 400 years. The interior consists of one small cosy bar with a pool table, two TVs plus a large screen projector for live sports. A choice of four real ales are available which includes Elgood's Cambridge at 3.8%, and three changing guest ales that are about abv 4%, 4.5% and one strong ale at around abv 5%. Cask cider is available from Addlestones. Opening hours are Mon-Sat 12-12.30am & Sun 12-10.30.

St. Johns Head

To complete the circuit, turn right out of St Johns Head and you will soon be back at "The Seafood Restaurant" where you turn left and cross the girder bridge back to Gt Yarmouth Railway Station.

The Haven Bridge

Breydon Water

Great Yarmouth Pub Walk

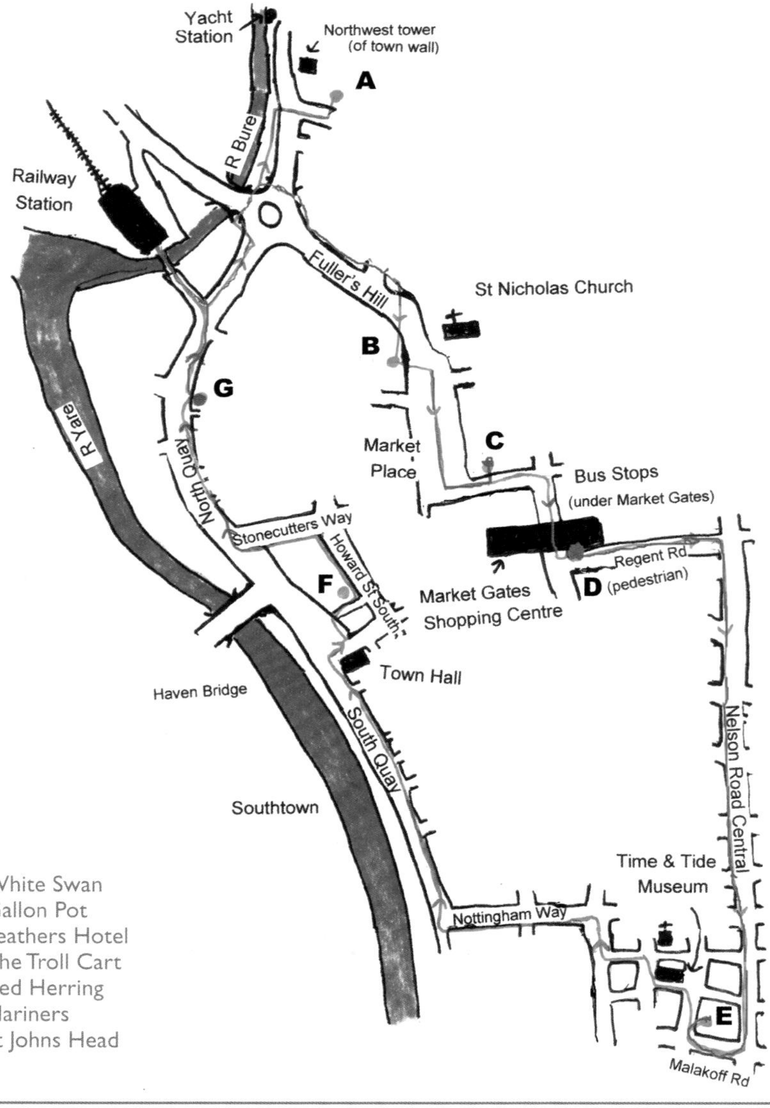

Yacht Station

Northwest tower (of town wall)

A

R Bure

Railway Station

Fuller's Hill

St Nicholas Church

B

Market Place

C

Bus Stops (under Market Gates)

G

R Yare

North Quay

Stonecutters Way

Howard St South

F

Market Gates Shopping Centre

Regent Rd (pedestrian)

D

Town Hall

Haven Bridge

South Quay

Nelson Road Central

Southtown

Time & Tide Museum

Nottingham Way

E

Malakoff Rd

A White Swan
B Gallon Pot
C Feathers Hotel
D The Troll Cart
E Red Herring
F Mariners
G St Johns Head

The Norwich Beer Festival

One of the highlights of Norwich & Norfolk's CAMRA Branch year is our annual Beer Festival. The first festival was in 1977, a small affair which took place in Blackfriars Hall.

Later the festival moved into the adjacent St Andrews Hall and has been going from strength to strength ever since. Over the years it has grown to take over St Andrews Hall, The Cloisters and most recently a marquee has been erected selling mainly continental bottled beers.

The festival takes place annually in late October, runs for a week and attracts over 15,000 visitors. There are usually over 200 different cask beers and around 25 ciders and perrys available.

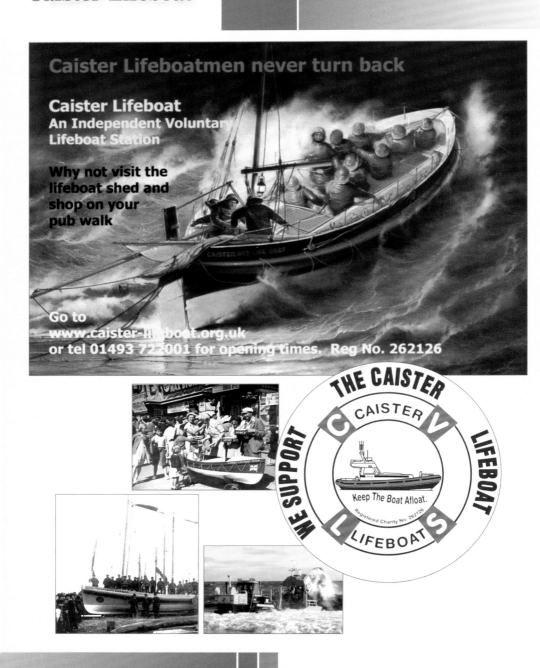

THE WOLF BREWERY

Award Winning Beers from the Heart of Norfolk

Call to book an educational and entertaining

BREWERY TOUR

For beers & souvenirs visit our

GIFT SHOP

The Wolf Brewery, Besthorpe, Attleborough
01953 457775   www.wolfbrewery.com

It takes all sorts to campaign for real ale

Save money by paying by Direct Debit

Join **CAMRA today...**

Complete the Direct Debit form below and you will receive three months membership free and a fantastic discount on your membership subscription. Alternatively you can send a cheque payable to **CAMRA** Ltd with your completed form, visit www.camra.org.uk or call 01727 867201. All forms should be addressed to Membership Secretary, CAMRA, 230 Hatfield Road, St Albans, AL1 4LW.

Your Details

Title .... Surname ....

Forename(s) ....

Date of Birth (dd/mm/yyyy) ....

Address ....

....

.... Postcode ....

Email address ....

Tel No (s) ....

Partner's Details (if Joint Membership)

Title .... Surname ....

Forename(s) ....

Date of Birth (dd/mm/yyyy) ....

Please state which CAMRA newsletter you found this form in? ....

	Direct Debit	Non DD
Single Membership (UK & EU)	£20	£22
Joint Membership (Partner at the same address)	£25	£27

For Young Member and concessionary rates please visit **www.camra.org.uk** or call **01727 867201**.

I wish to join the Campaign for Real Ale, and agree to abide by the Memorandum and Articles of Association.

I enclose a cheque for ....

Signed .... Date ....

Applications will be processed within 21 days

Mem Form 0108

Instruction to your Bank or Building Society to pay by Direct Debit

DIRECT Debit

Please fill in the form and send to: **Campaign for Real Ale Ltd.** 230 Hatfield Road, St Albans, Herts AL1 4LW

Name and full postal address of your Bank or Building Society

To the Manager   Bank or Building Society

Address

Postcode

Name(s) of Account Holder (s)

Bank or Building Society Account Number

Branch Sort Code

Reference Number

Originators Identification Number

9	2	6	1	2	9

FOR CAMRA OFFICIAL USE ONLY
This is not part of the instruction to your Bank or Building Society

Membership Number

Name

Postcode

Instructions to your Bank or Building Society
Please pay CAMRA Direct Debits from the account detailed on this instruction subject to the safeguards assured by the Direct Debit Guarantee. I understand that this instruction may remain with CAMRA and, if so will be passed electronically to my Bank/Building Society.

Signature(s)

Date

Banks and Building Societies may not accept Direct Debit Instructions for some types of account.

DIRECT Debit

This Guarantee should be detached and retained by the payer.

The Direct Debit Guarantee

- This Guarantee is offered by all Banks and Building Societies that take part in the Direct Debit Scheme. The efficiency and security of the Scheme is monitored and protected by your own Bank or Building Society.
- If the amounts to be paid or the payment dates change CAMRA will notify you 10 working days in advance of your account being debited or as otherwise agreed.
- If an error is made by CAMRA or your Bank or Building Society, you are guaranteed a full and immediate refund from your branch of the amount paid.
- You can cancel a Direct Debit at any time by writing to your Bank or Building Society. Please also send a copy of your letter to us.

detached and retained this section